iPad Air 4th Generation 2020 User Manual

A Beginner to Pro Guide to Master the New iPad Air 4

DANIEL STONE

Copyright

Contents

Chapter One

The most recent iPad Air feels like the exceptional tablet we've been demanding from Apple for quite a long time; a tablet with a cutting edge plan and bigger screen like the Pro. It's the most preferred iPad in Apple's arrangement for the individuals who need an all-round tablet for the purpose of entertainment, coupled with productivity. Preceding tablets like the original iPad were designed to have a more ideal screen for doing a significant number of the things individuals had just barely begun doing regularly on their cell phones, such as watching videos, perusing the web, and sending messages. However, sequel to the launch of Microsoft's Windows 8 software in 2012, PC manufacturers started making tablets equipped for filling in as reasonable PC substitutions.

Apple's new $600 iPad Air is designed to be in the middle of this range. It's not in any way a replacement for a laptop, nor is it the regular type of tablet designed mostly for media consumption. The iPad Air is a device Apple is designed to be in between the Apple's lineup of the $329 basic iPad and the iPad Pro, which starts at $800 for the 11-inch model.

Features of the iPad Air

Design

The iPad Air is built with an entirely revamped look with a larger screen that is nearly borderless which gives it a more premium look. Just like the iPad Pro, the iPad Air also has slimmer bezels and flat edges, an aesthetic that can be seen among the latest iPhones as well.

Coming to the front side, the iPad Air is embedded with a large 10.9-inch 2,360 x 1,640 resolution display, this delivers absolutely well in terms of viewing experience, which is vital due to the fact that the screen is probably the most important feature of any tablet.

Security

The catchy aspect of the iPad Air's design is that it's Apple's only mobile device to retain Touch ID even without the home button. Instead, Apple's fingerprint scanner is positioned in the top button. For easier and quicker unlocking, a useful addition in the iPad Air is the face unlock that enables you to quickly unlock the iPad even when you're putting on a face mask or the tablet is positioned in a way that isn't directly in line with your eyes.

Another aspect of the iPad Air's design that seems different this time is the color options. This mid-tier device from Apple comes in silver, space gray, rose gold, green, and blue, providing it with a more lively look compared to earlier iPad models.

The iPad Air's design is basically an all-screen design that entails a large 10.9-inch Liquid Retina display for an enthralling visual experience, with 3.8 million pixels and sophisticated technologies, such as full lamination, P3 wide color support, True Tone, and an anti-reflective coating for an amazing visual experience

Furthermore, the iPad Air comes with a USB-C port instead of Lightning, enabling faster data transfer and a more extensive compatibility with non-Apple accessories, and support for Apple's new Magic Keyboard and second-generation iPad Pencil.

Performance

Being a recent device, it is expected to have the latest processor and that is how it is. The iPad Air is embedded with the new A14 Bionic processor. With this processor, the iPad Air exhibits a significant boost in performance, handling even the most power-consuming apps. The

A14 Bionic makes editing 4K videos relatively easier for users thereby creating astonishing works of art, playing immersive games, and more. This processor is built utilizing a 5nm manufacturing process which provides users with better performance without heavily consuming battery life. With this 5-nanometer process technology, A14 Bionic is developed with about 11.8 billion transistors for increased performance and power efficiency in almost all parts of the chip. Moreover, this latest-generation A-series chip entails a new 6-core design for a huge 40 percent boost in CPU performance, and a new 4-core graphics architecture for about 30 percent improvement in graphics.

Storage

The iPad Air comes with two variants when it comes to storage capacity, there's the 64GB variant and 256GB variant. These two variants definitely do not have the same price as the 64GB variant costs $600 while the 256GB variant is priced at $750

Camera

The iPad Air is built with a 7-megapixel front-facing camera rather than the basic model's 1.2-megapixel selfie camera. By implication, making FaceTime calls on the iPad Air appears to be much crisper and more detailed than those made on the regular iPad. Turning this gadget over, there's a 12-megapixel wide camera that can shoot 4K video, mostly very useful and handy for video editors and students that intend to shoot videos, and perform a bit of editing on the same device while working remotely.

Battery

According to Apple, the iPad Air has a talk time of about 10 hours, even when connected to Wi-Fi,

According to Apple, the iPad Air has a talk time of about 10 hours, even when connected to Wi-Fi,

The iPad Air

How to Set Up iPad

When it comes to setting up an iPad, it is essential that you understand your options

After powering the device, you'll come across the following options and this is what they stand for;

Set up as new - this implies that you're starting everything , the entire setting, from scratch. This is aimed at people who are just using a smartphone or online services for the very first time.

Restore from a previous iPhone, iPad, or iPod touch backup. This can be done online with iCloud or over USB with iTunes. This is meant for people who initially had an iOS device and are moving to a new one, in this case, an iPad Air.

Import from Android, BlackBerry, or Windows Phone. There's an application in Google Play that is developed by Apple to make moving data and files from an Android easier. However, online services enable you to transfer a large amount of data over from any old device.

Irrespective of the option you select or the one that applies to you, everything goes through the same process.Touch slide to initiate the set up and, as it is stated on the screen, slide your finger across the screen to begin the process.

- Select your preferred language option. If you purchased your iPad Air in your native country, the appropriate language related will be automatically selected.

- Pick the region or country you are presently. In the same manner, this is by default set to the place where you purchased the gadgets if you live in that region.

-Select a Wi-Fi network and input its password, if inquired. In instances whereby there's no Wi-Fi around, you can switch to use Cellular instead for an iPad with data.

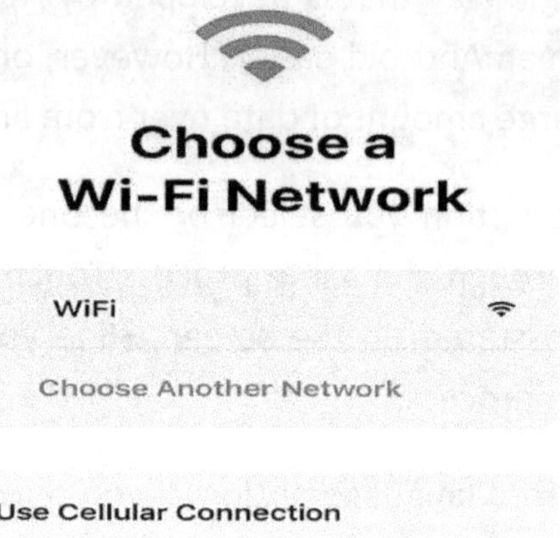

- Hold on for a few seconds for your iPhone or iPad to activate.

-Set whether you want the Location Services to be enabled or not. You can always adjust this option later, however, it is necessary that you enable at least some location services to use apps like Maps.

- Input up your Passcode, and set your touch ID and face ID. This part can be skipped at that moment by pressing "Set Up Touch ID Later."

How to Backup iPad on macOS Big Sur

First thing you need to do is to connect your iPad to your Mac via a Lighting cable. Then, open a window in the Finder on your Mac, this can easily be done via Command-N.

Move to the Locations section situated at the left column of the Finder window, go through it to check for your device and click on it. Details about your device will be displayed in the right side of the window.

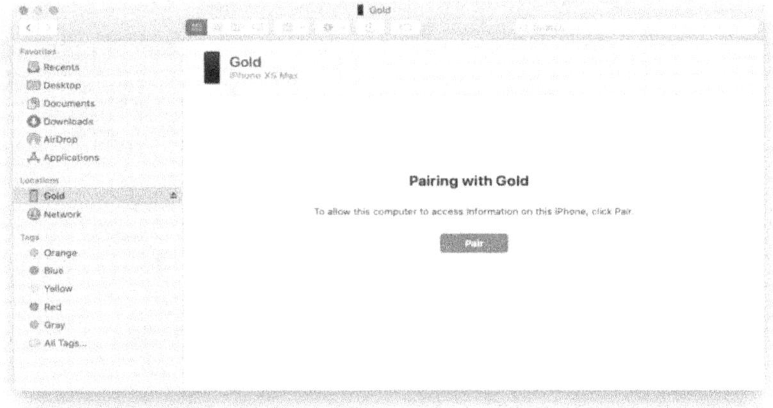

Afterwards, click on the General button positioned at the crest of the window. After clicking the button, glance through for the section termed "Backups". At this point, there are a few options you have to consider:

-You can decide to back up "your most important data" to iCloud, or you back up the entirety of your device's data to your Mac.

-Incase you intend to encrypt the files you backup on your Mac, you can do this by selecting "Encrypt local backup."

With those in place, when you are ready to complete the backup process, press the "Back Up Now" button. Likewise, you can click the "Sync" button at the base of the window. And that is all, your files are now backed up.

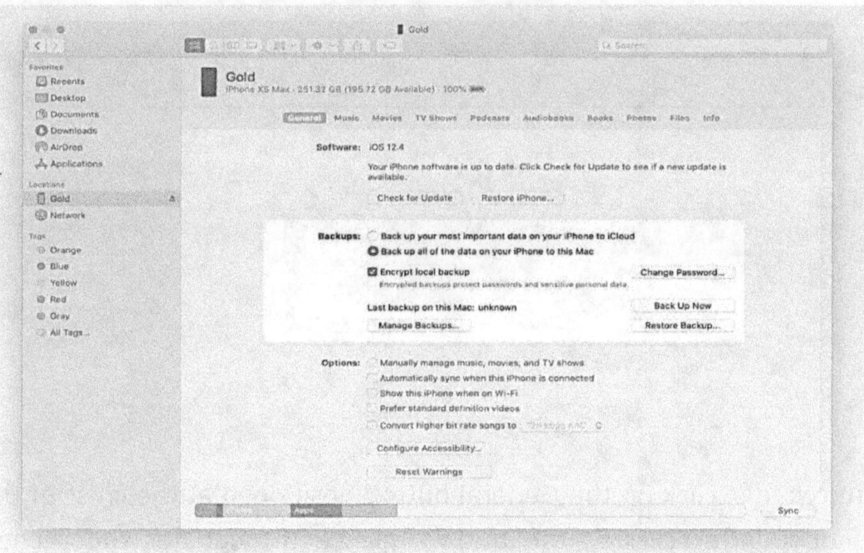

How to Restore your iPad on macOS

If the need to restore your iPad utilizing a backup on your Mac arises, here's how you can go about it;

Firstly, interface your iPad with your Mac via a Lighting cable. Afterwards, open a window in the Finder (Command-N). Similarly, the section that is labelled "Location" in the left column of the Finder window, search for your device and click on it. Information pertaining to your device will be displayed on the right side of the window. As usual, press the General button at the crest of the window. Afterwards, glance through till you find the section labelled as "Backups". Click on the Restore Backup button, doing this will cause a window to be displayed. In this window, you will select which of the backups you intend to use for the restore process. If you press the pop-up menu tagged as "backup," you can select which backup you intend to use.

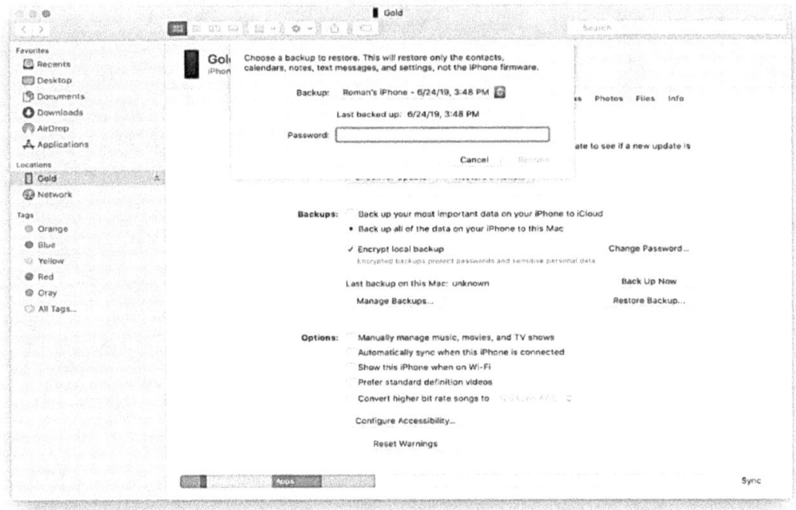

Then, input your password, and click Restore to initiate the process. The entire process might take a few minutes before it is completed.

Restore from iCloud backup

This process should be done when you are setting up your iPad, if your iPad has already been set up, you need to wipe the entire content on it before you can utilize these steps to restore from your backup. Power the device, and a "Hello" screen will be displayed, adhere to the onscreen setup steps until you get to Apps & Data screen, then press "Restore from iCloud Backup". Then, sign in to iCloud with your Apple ID and select a backup. Check the date and size of each and select the ones that are most relevant at that moment. When you are done selecting, the transfer begins

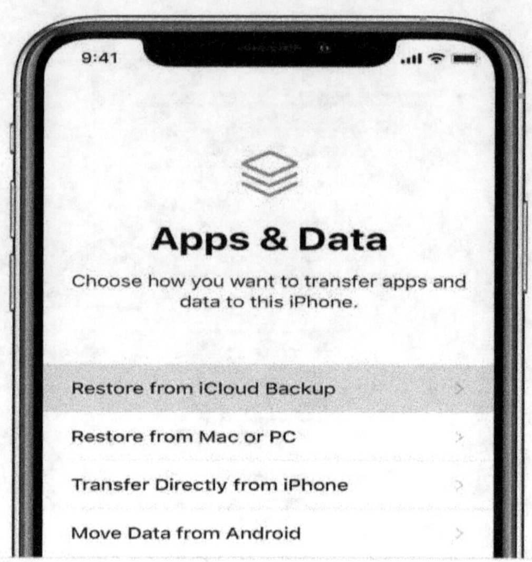

It is compulsory that you have an active internet connection as this is what will fuel the restore process in the first place. Ensure that you are always connected to the Wi-Fi or cellular data connection, then hang on for the progress bar to appear and be completed.

The progress bar might be completed within a few minutes, or more than an hour contingent upon the size of the backup and the network speed. If, by any chance, you disconnect from Wi-Fi during the process, the progress will pause until you are actively connected to the internet again. When the progress bar completes, you can finish setup and start exploring your device. In addition, content like your apps, photos, music, and other information will keep on being restored in the background for the next couple of hours or days, contingent upon the amount of information you are restoring.

Turn on iCloud Backup

In the home screen, press the settings icon. Afterwards click on   [your name] > iCloud > iCloud Backup. When you tap the iCloud toggle, it activates iCloud Backup. By implication, iCloud constantly backs up your iPad regularly when the iPad is plugged to a power source, locked, and on Wi-Fi. If you tap that iCloud Backup toggle again, it turns this feature off.

If you intend to carry out a manual backup, tap Back Up Now. In case you want to take a look at your iCloud backups, go to Settings > [your name] > iCloud > Manage Storage > Backups. You can likewise delete a backup from the list , select that backup, and then press "Delete Backup".

How to Reset iPad

There are different sorts of resets on iPad, it could be performed via any of these three methods:

-Shut Down: This option can be found at the base of the General menu in the Settings app, it switches off your iPad. After shutting the iPad down, you can then switch it on via the power button. "Rebooting" a lagging iPad in this manner has often turned out to be the easiest way to fix an app that is responsible for that glitch.

-Reset all settings: Just like the name implies, this option reverts the entirety of iPad's settings to their defaults, but none of your content will be erased. This reset option is present in the Settings app, and can be activated by pressing "General" in the settings app, and then Reset.

-The third and ultimate option is the Factory Reset. When you carry out a factory reset, otherwise referred to as "Erase All Content and Settings" , in the iPad's Settings app, the entire information and content present on the iPad will be wiped off. This makes the iPad appear as new as the way it was when you purchased it.

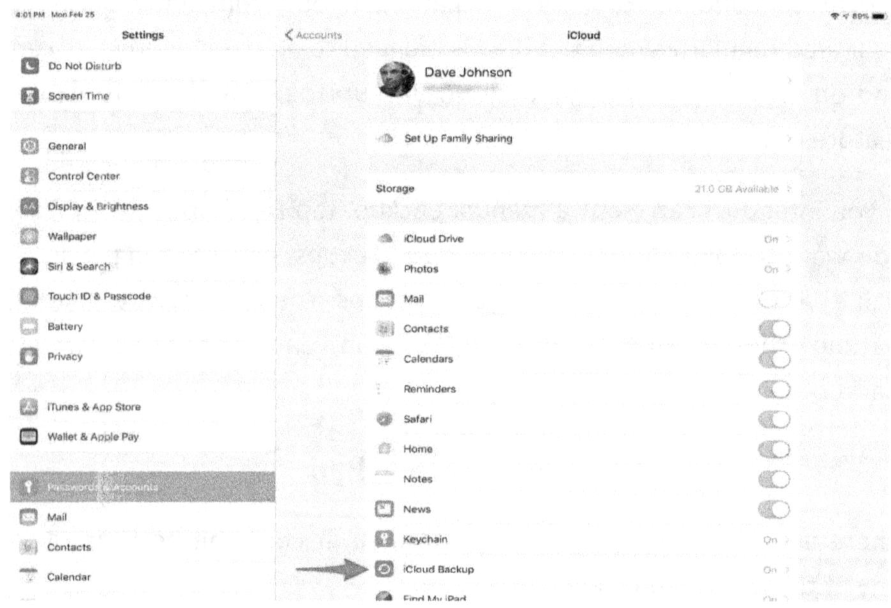

It is advisable that you backup your iPad to iCloud first before carrying out the factory reset in case you intend to restore the content of the iPad, either to the same iPad or to a different one. This can be done in the Settings app by selecting " Passwords & Accounts", then press iCloud Backup, and tapping Back Up Now, as shown in the image below.

To carry out the factory reset, press the settings app icon in the home screen and tap "General". From there, press "Reset" and select "Erase All Content and Settings"

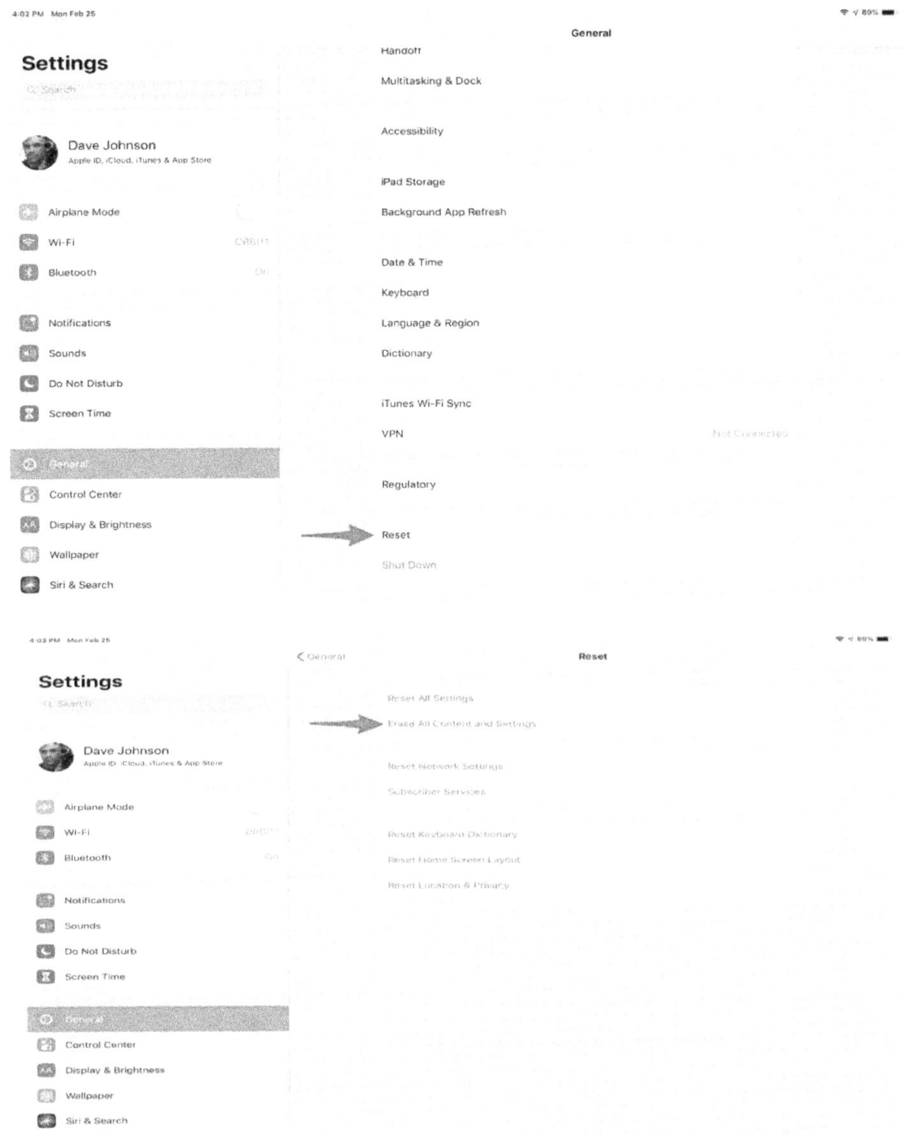

Then press "Backup Then Erase" if you want to create duplicates of the iPad's content before the reset takes place, however this is not needed if you've backed it up earlier. You can go ahead and press "Erase Now" if the content of your iPad has been backed up. Afterwards, input your iPad's password to confirm where it is required and continue. All you have to do now is to sit back and watch the factory reset take place. When it's done, your iPad will seem to be the way it was when you first brought it home from the store, and it displays the initial setup screen.

How to Create a New Apple ID

During the process of setting up on your new iPad, you might be inquired to put in your Apple ID and password. Peradventure you haven't registered an Apple ID, you can create a new one as you set up the iPad Air. This can also be done in the Application store later.

If you intend to do this during the set up, press "Forgot password" or "Don't have an Apple ID". Afterwards, select "Create a Free Apple ID". Fill in the required details in the screen that is displayed, and press Next. At this point, choose "Use your current email address", or select "Get a free iCloud email address".

Chapter Two

Set up Apple Pay

Apple Pay is an application that enables you to carry out in-store purchases and online purchases with your iPad, all that is needed is a touch of the Home button and a scan of your fingerprint. Apple pay makes purchases made with the credit and debit cards easier and more secure.

How to add a card for Apple Pay

On the home screen, tap the Wallet app to open it. Then, press the + button shown at the edge of your screen. Afterwards, press Continue or Next on the Apple Pay screen.

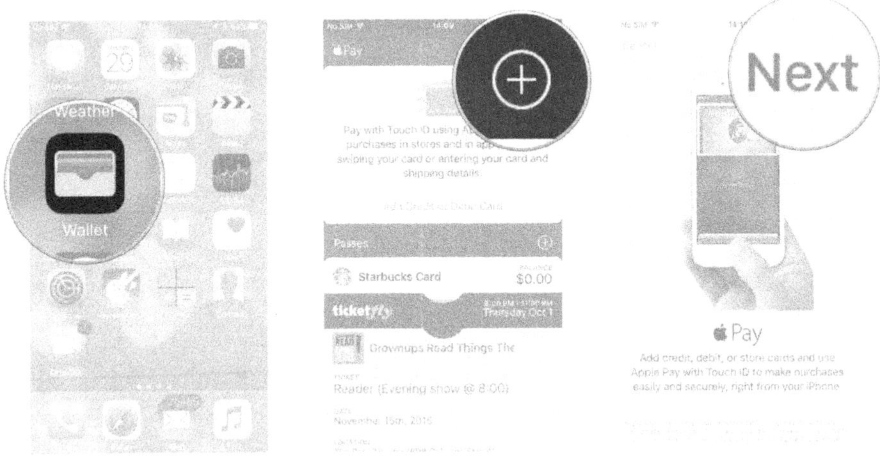

Type in your credit or debit card details, or just scan the card with your iPad's camera. Proceed by pressing Next on the Card Details screen.

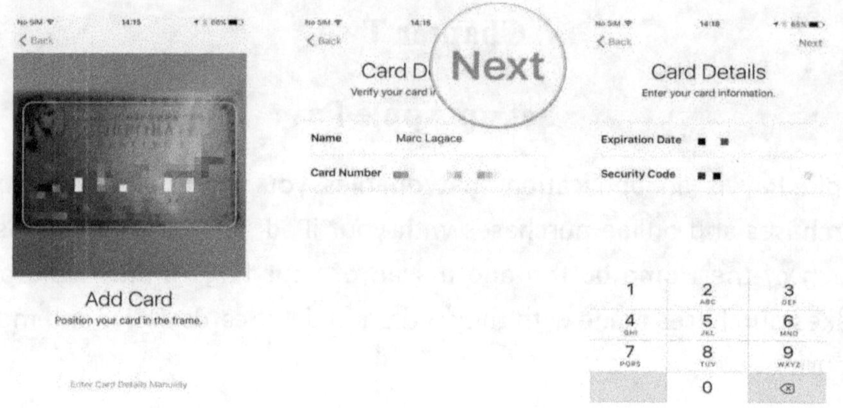

The next screen inquires whether you agree to the terms and conditions, you can go through the terms and conditions if you want but in order to move on, you have to press "Agree" which affirms that you accept the terms and conditions

At this point, a verification method will be displayed, select the method you prefer, and press "Enter Code".

Input the verification code that you are provided with. This depends on the choice of the verification method you made earlier on, it could be email, text, or call.

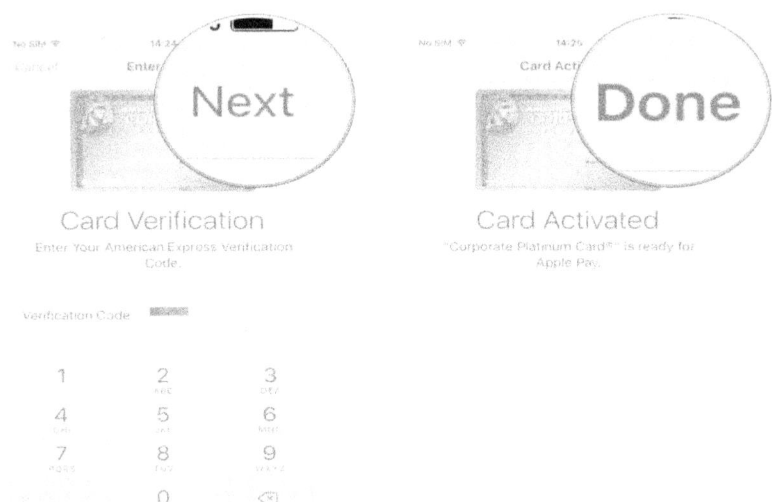

Afterwards, press Done to wrap up the entire process

How to authorize a card for Apple Pay

The needed procedures to authorize a card for Apple Pay may differ based on the bank. For instance, certain banks automatically add and activate your card for Apple Pay as soon as you accept the terms and conditions. Others might demand an activation code. Furthermore, if your mobile banking application is present on your iPad, it might be possible to launch the app to authorize your card.

How to change the default card for Apple Pay

Apple Pay is dynamic in the sense that it permits you to use more than one credit and debit card, this enables you to easily switch between them whenever the need to do so arise. Nevertheless, the default credit or debit card still retains the attributes of being the fastest and easiest to use. Hence, it is advisable that you make your main card the default card. To make the changes, open the Settings app on your iPad and move to Wallet & Apple Pay. Afterwards, press Default Card and select the card you want to use as your default.

Tap Wallet & Apple Pay in Settings, tap Default Card, and select the card you want to use as default

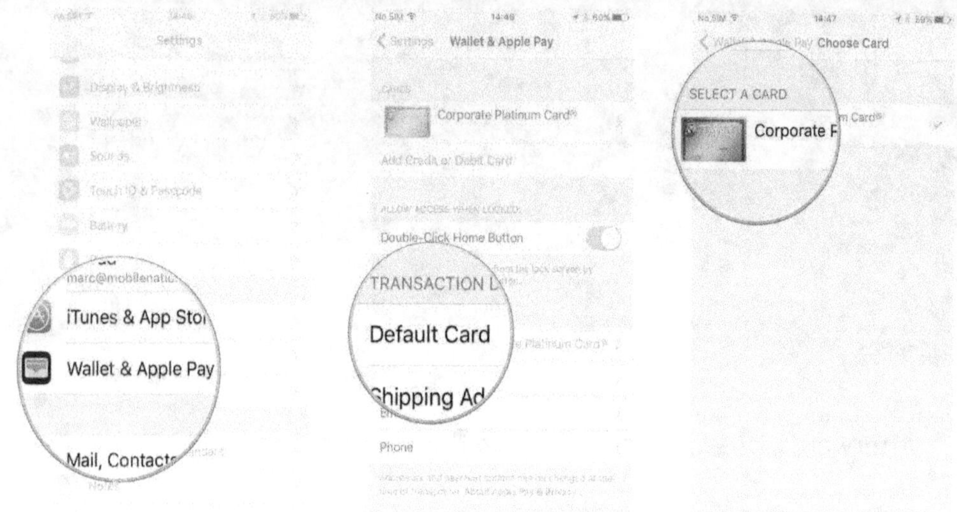

How to remove a card from Apple Pay

In Apple pay, it is easy to bring in any, and the entirety of your supported credit and debit cards. However, in case you misplace, cancel, or change a card for any reason, you'll need to remove it. This is how to go about it:

Go to the Settings app on your iPad that has the Apple Pay card you intend to delete, press Wallet & Apple Pay. The credit card you intend to remove, scroll down and press "Remove This Card"

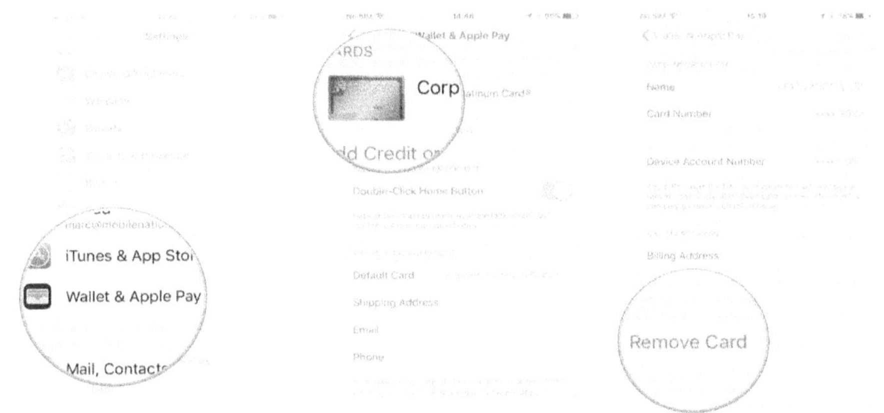

The card you deleted will from that moment cease to be eligible for use with Apple Pay on that particular device.

How to Use Apple Cash Family

Apple cash family is a feature on Apple devices that's exclusive to iOS 14. The feature enables parents to set up Apple Cash for their wards (children and teens). Apple cash entails limits, notifications, and the enablement to lock an account.

Requirements for using Apple Cash Family

Since your iPad Air comes with iOS 14 installed on it, it is compatible with Apple Pay. In order to use Apple Cash Family, you must have initially used Family Sharing and have a family member whose age is below 18. If you happen to be the family organizer, it is compulsory that you use the same Apple ID you used when you set up Family Sharing. That being said, members of a family group must:

- Have their own suitable Apple device which has the latest version of iOS, iPadOS, or watchOS installed on it.

- Each member will then Sign in to iCloud on their device via their Apple ID.

-Have two-factor authentication activated for each Apple ID.

-Set the region on their device to the United States.

Set up Apple Cash Family for a child or teen

To put the Apple Cash Family to use, on the family organizer's iPhone, go to settings. Then, press your name at the top of the settings list, and select Family Sharing. At this point, select Apple Cash, and choose your ward. Now, press Set Up Apple Cash.

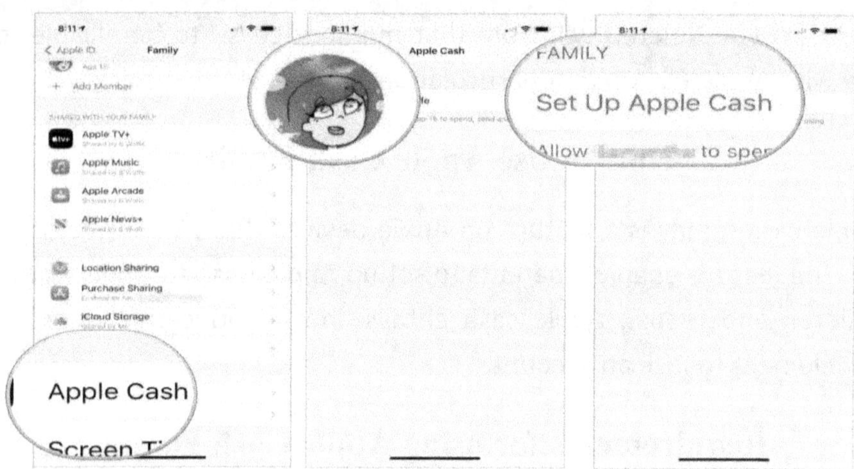

If you're at this point, press Continue and select the contacts that can be sent Apple Cash via Messages by your wards. Your choice of selection could be " Everyone", "Contacts Only", or "Family Members Only". The good thing here is you can change your choice of selection at any time. Proceed and agree to the Terms and Conditions, you might read it if you want to.

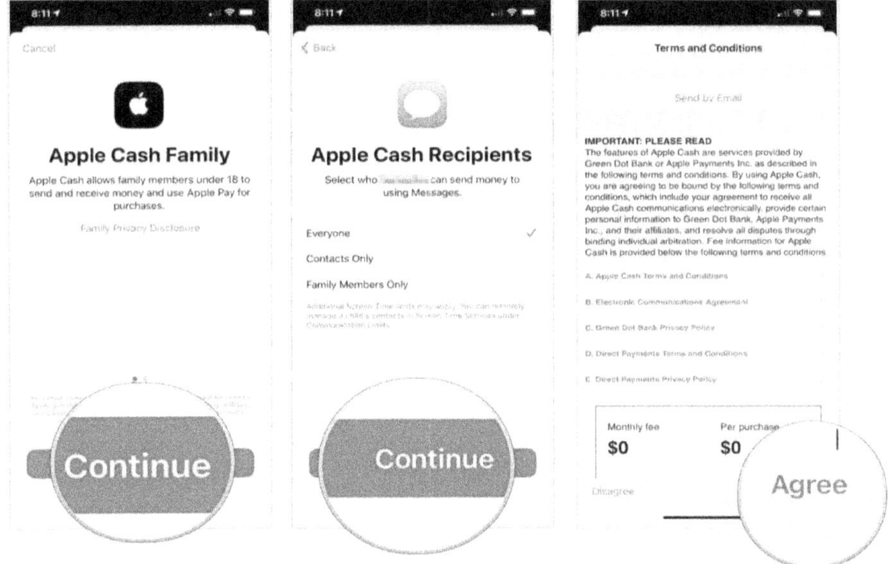

Adhere to the guidelines that will be displayed on your screen to set up the Apple Cash Family account. A sort of identity verification might be demanded. In the event that it displays "Pending", recheck to ensure your ward satisfies the requirements. Your wards will be able to make use of Apple Cash just like every other person, with the restrictions you set still active.

To view Apple Cash Family transactions:

Press your Apple Cash card in the Wallet app on your iPad, afterwards press the "More" button. Move down and press your ward's name. There are numerous options here, contingent upon whether you're the Family Organizer or a parent/guardian.

As the family organizer for Apple Cash Family, you are allowed to:

-   View your child's Apple Cash balance and transactions. You can as well select who your child can carry out transactions with. Furthermore, you can activate "Notify Me" so you are notified about any transaction made by your family members.

Also, you can Lock Apple Cash to prevent your child from making purchases or sending and receiving money in Messages.

Sending money with Apple pay cash on messages

Sending money to your friends and family in Messages is somewhat similar to sending a sticker. Ensure you have set up your Apple pay cash, then simply open Messages on your iPad. On that contact you intend to send money to, press the conversation with the person or press start a new iMessage conversation if you don't have an initial conversation. Afterwards, press the Apple Pay button placed at the base of the screen.

At this point, press the − or + buttons to select the amount to send, alternatively, you can press "Show Keypad " if you intend to input a specific amount, and then input the amount.

Now, all you need to do is to press Pay. Press the send button and then, authorize the payment from an Apple Pay-linked debit card.

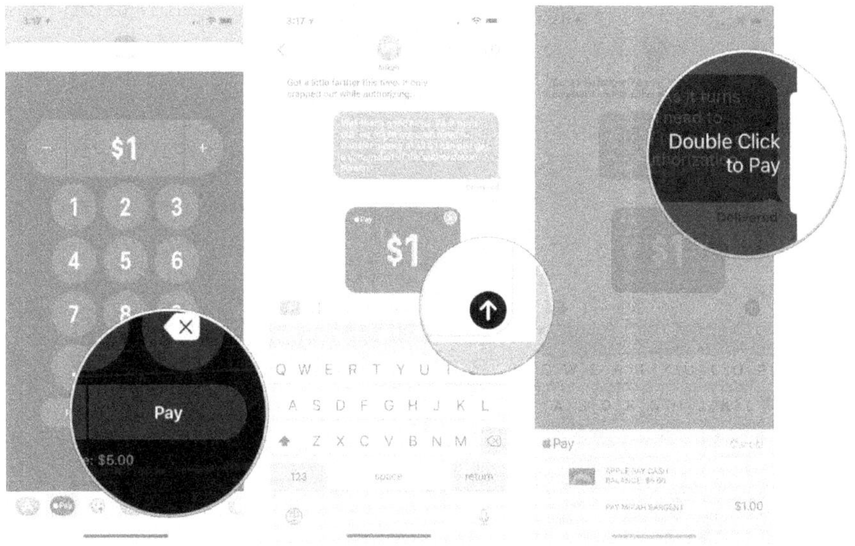

How to add money to your Apple Pay Cash card

Open the Wallet application on your iPad, and press your Apple Pay Cash card. Afterwards, press the more info icon (•••) at the edge of the screen.

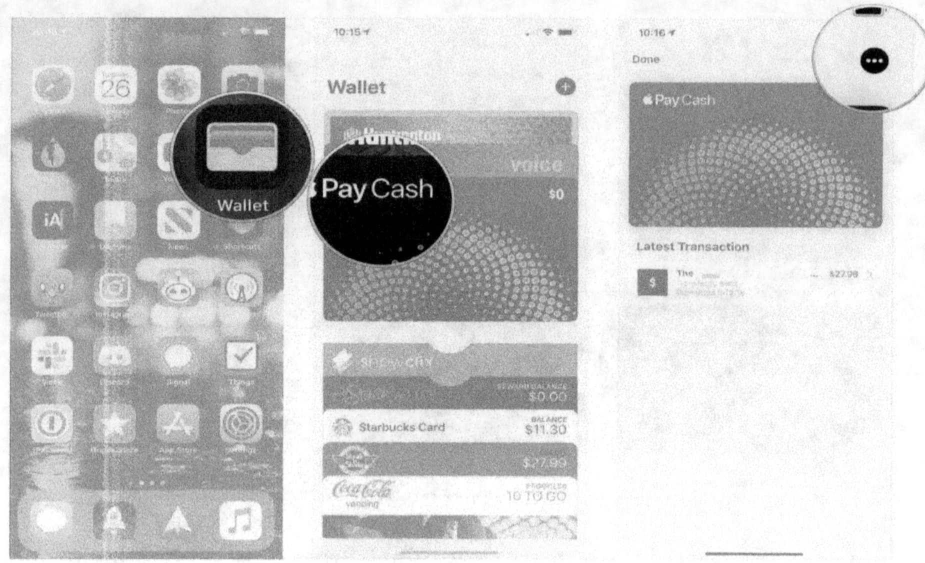

At this point, press Add Money and input the amount of money you want to add to your card by utilizing either the default buttons or by inputting a custom amount on the number pad.

Afterwards, press Add and confirm the transfer from an Apple Pay-linked debit card either with the touch ID or face ID.

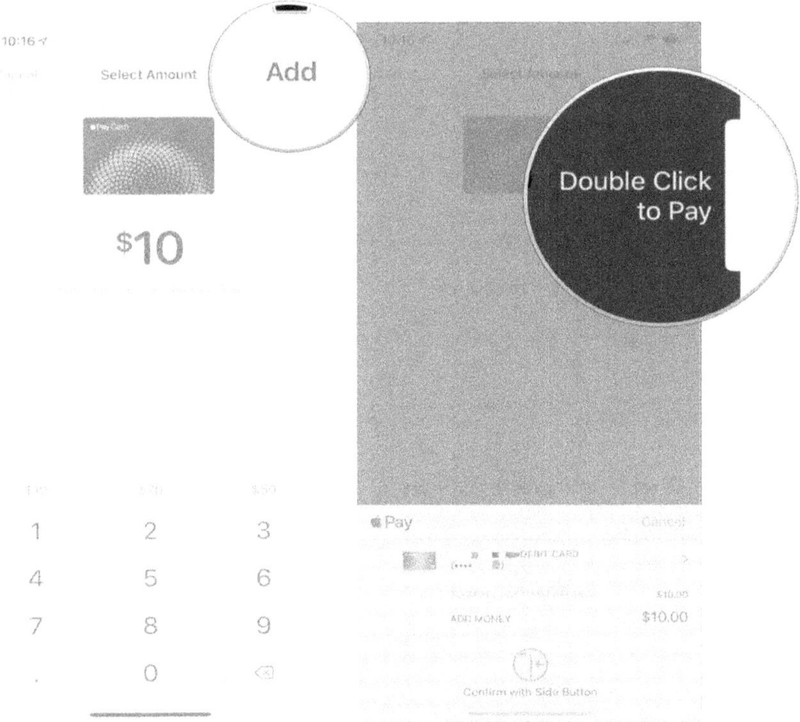

How to verify your identity for Apple Pay

To guarantee a hitch-free process of using Apple Pay Cash, it is essential that you verify your identity. Go to Settings on your iPad and select "Wallet & Apple Pay". Then to Apple Pay Cash.

Afterwards, press Verify Identity, and Continue. Input your personal details as required

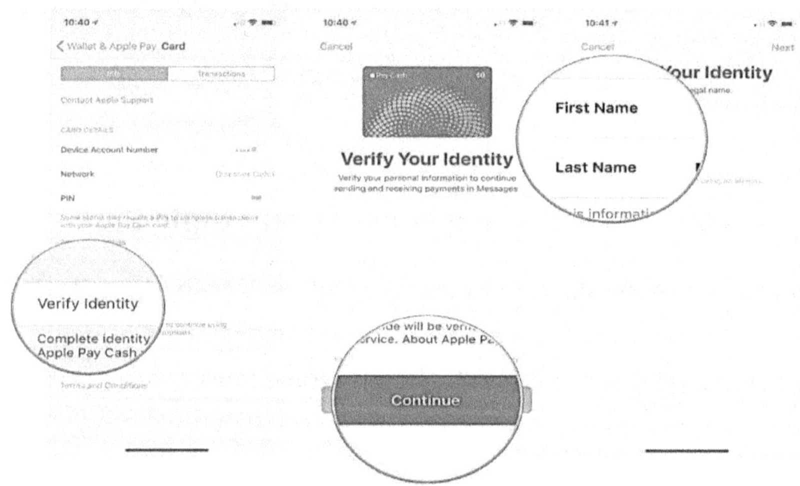

Press Next and input your address, then proceed.

Next, input the appropriate details where needed and proceed.

How to send your Apple Pay Cash balance to a bank account

Any money that is sent to your Apple Pay Cash card can be sent from your card to any bank account of your choice. Go to Wallet on your iPad, and press your Apple Pay Cash card. Then press the more info icon (•••) at the edge of the screen.

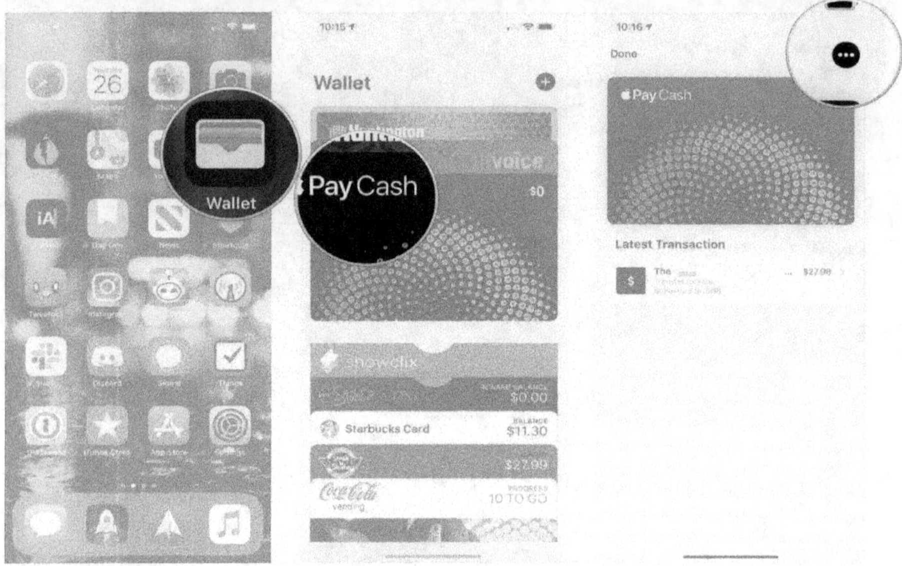

Afterwards, select Transfer to Bank and fill in the amount that you intend to send from your Apple Pay Cash balance to that bank account, and proceed.

Select either Instant Transfer or 1-3 Business Days. The only difference is that Instant Transfer charges you a transfer fee and requires a debit card, while 1-3 Business Days only needs you to fill in your bank account details. Press transfer, and authorize the transaction.

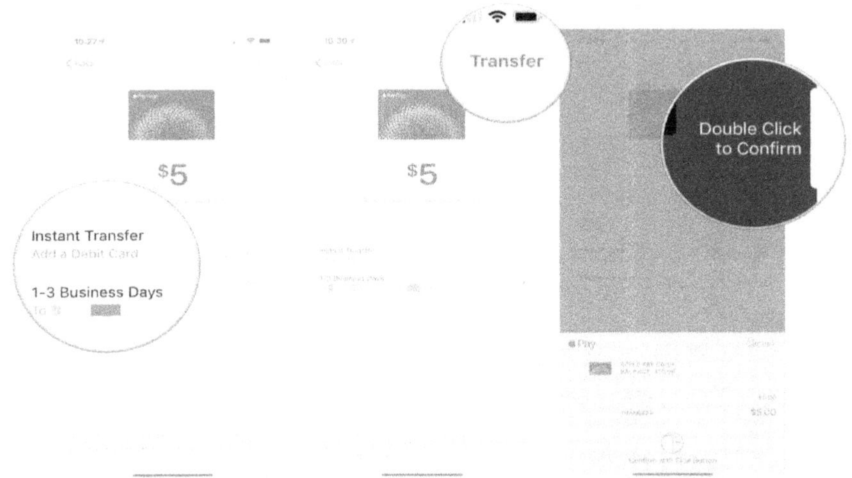

How to request a payment with Apple Pay Cash

Definitely, you can as well request a payment through Messages. Simply go to the Messages app on your iPad, and press the conversation with the contact you intend to request money from or initiate a new iMessage conversation. Then, press the Apple Pay button positioned at the base of the screen.

At this point, press the − or + buttons to select an amount, alternatively you can press Show Keypad if you prefer to fill in a specific amount. Input the amount and proceed.

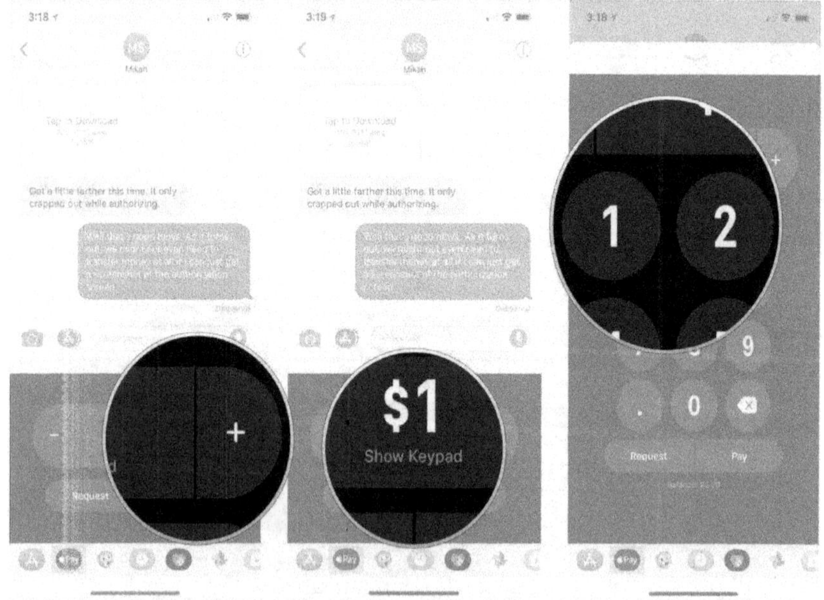

Now, press Request and then the send button.

$1
1 2 3
4 5 6
7 8 9
Request
Balance:

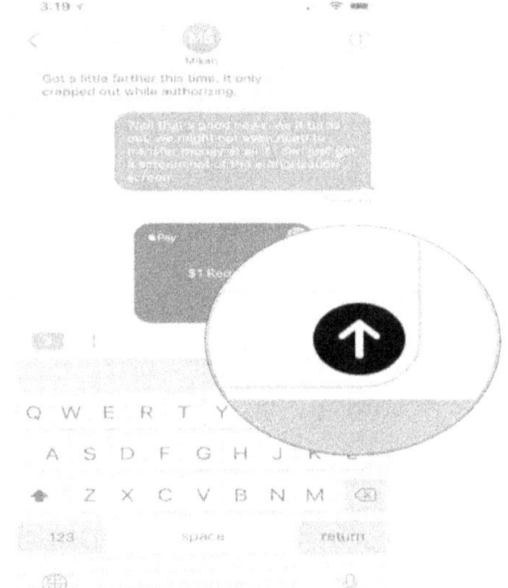
Mikah
Got a little farther this time. It only crapped out while authorizing.
Pay
$1 Req
Q W E R T Y
A S D F G H J K
Z X C V B N M
123   space   return

<h1 style="text-align:center">Chapter Three</h1>

<h2 style="text-align:center">How to Use a wireless or USB mouse</h2>

Connecting a Bluetooth Mouse

Firstly, ensure your Bluetooth mouse is near your device and is sufficiently charged. Then, on your iPad, go to Settings > Accessibility > Touch. At this point, select assistive Touch and switch it on. Move down to "Pointer Devices" and select "Devices."

Afterwards, select "Bluetooth Devices" to initiate the pairing process. Now set your Bluetooth mouse to discoverable (or pairing mode) and tap on its name when it shows up on your iPad or iPhone.

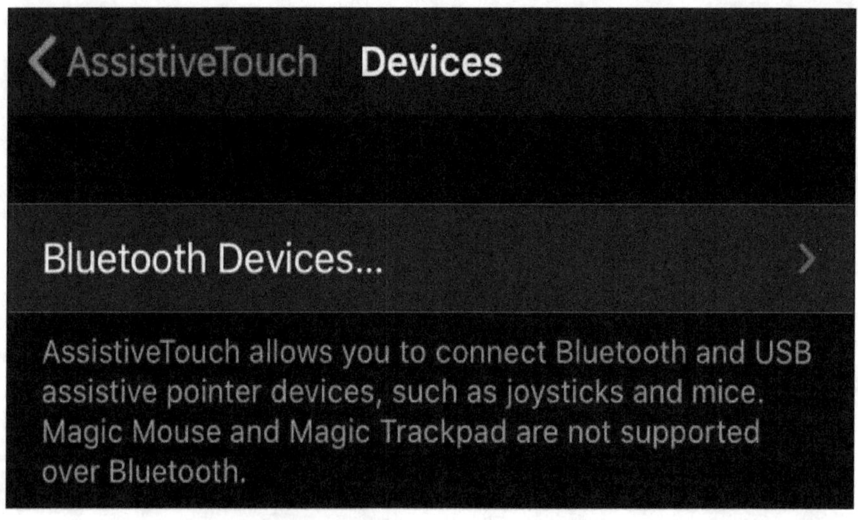

<h2 style="text-align:center">Connecting a USB Mouse</h2>

To interface a usb mouse to your iPad, you have to get Apple's Lightning to camera USB cable. This accessory was primarily designed to send images from a digital camera to your device's internal storage.

However, if you have an iPad with a USB Type-C adapter and a suitable mouse, you can just plug it in directly.

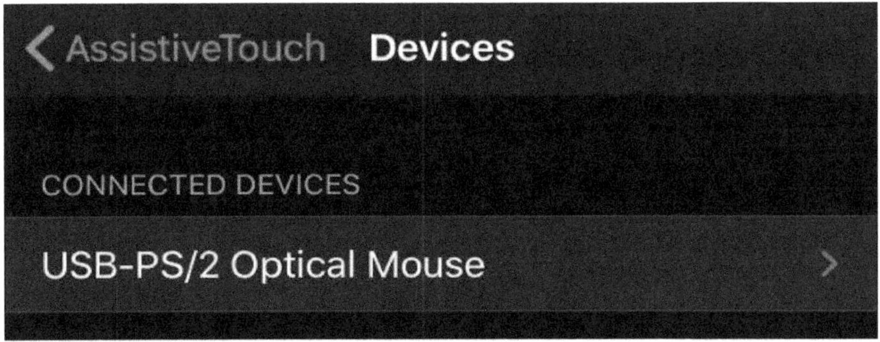

Insert the USB to the USB port of your mouse, and then connect the Lightning jack to your iPad. Next, move to Settings > Accessibility > Touch. Press "Assistive Touch" and activate it.

Tips for Using the mouse

- **Customizing pointer appearance**

In case you're finding it somewhat difficult to spot the round pointer as you move it across the iPad screen, you can simply adjust the size, and even assign another color to the pointer to ensure it is distinct from the background. In addition to making the pointer larger, you can likewise adjust its contrast and change stroke size for pointer outline. To make these changes, go to settings → Accessibility → Pointer Control.

- **Accessing iOS features faster**

With a mouse to your support, features on your iPad like the Control or Notification Center , the app switcher are made relatively easier. For instance, to get to the Control Center, you just move the pointer to select the iOS status icons in the top edge of the screen, and then you click. Alternatively, you might not even need to click at all, simply swipe the pointer past a screen section with your finger, this brings in a feature, afterwards, swipe the pointer past the edge of the screen again.

For instance, you can bring in your Notification Center by highlighting the status icons on iPad in the top-left corner with the pointer, then click. Or, on the other hand, you can just move the pointer with one finger past the top of the screen towards the center.

- **Use keyboard shortcuts**

Putting a pointing device like a mouse to use will instantly increase the productivity of your iPad however, this pointing device coupled with keyboard shortcuts gives you near optimum productivity. In the Safari application on your iPad, you can Control-click something to pull up the right-click function, which is useful if there's no secondary mouse button to carry out the right-click function. An image can be control-clicked to display the options to save it. Performing control-clicking on a link in Safari provides you with the contextual menu without also previewing the URL.

- **Right Clicking**

To activate right clicking for your mouse, press the Secondary Click portion just below the Mouse heading, then select the mouse button that you want to assign the right-click function. Right-clicking can be done to access contextual menus in a various applications, including right-clicking icons on the Home screen, in the Dock and so forth.

How to use the QuickTake feature

The QuickTake feature just as its name implies helps you to take multiple pictures or videos in a short time. After opening the Camera application on your iPad, what you'll see is the default photo mode. If you want to snap a picture, tap the Shutter button.

To capture a QuickTake picture or video, all you need to do is press and hold the Shutter button, and release the button when you're done. Alternatively, holding the Volume buttons when you're in the camera application can capture a QuickTake video. Also, you use the Volume Up button for Burst enabled, and you can capture a QuickTake video with the Volume down button.

How to use the new camera app

The new camera app on the iPad Air and every other Apple device with iOS 14 has some sort of new features embedded in it. Part of the changes is the included four blocks of controls, beginning with a large one to carry out nearly everything from the format in which you take the shots to a burst of shots can be taken. Other significant features are the Preserve Settings, and Use Volume Up for Burst. The Burst feature is relatively simpler, all you have to do is activate it, and the Burst Mode available will be available to you when you press the volume up button when the camera application is opened.

On the other hand, Preserve Settings is more complex. What it basically does is to instruct the Camera app to provide you with the same selections you made the last time you used it. For instance, if you shot video the previous time, the Camera app will open up ready to shoot video this time. Likewise, it can utilize the same aspect ratio, the same filters, and so on.

How to use the grid in iOS 14

The Camera app entails a three-by-three grid template to assist you with composing a shot before you take it. Although, the option to either activate or deactivate it is in the Composition section in Camera settings. The recent arrangement of Camera settings includes the ability to have it remember what you used previously.

It is coupled with a Mirror Front Camera which is either going to make you appear better or otherwise. With this enabled, your selfie shots will appear like looking in a mirror – they will be reversed.

How to Zoom In and Out on iPad

The Zoom feature on iPad enables the user to either zoom in (increase the size) the contents shown on the iPad screen. After you zoom in, you can as well zoom out again when you want the text and images to be displayed on-screen at their default size. After activating the zoom feature on the iPad, you simply double-tap the screen with three fingers to zoom in. You don't have to squint your eyes in order to see things clearly on your iPad, simply activate the Zoom, and utilize it when needed so you'll have a detailed view of what's on the screen.

Go to settings on your iPad, and press General. Then, select Accessibility in the general settings, the Accessibility options will be displayed. Next, tap Zoom so the Zoom options are displayed.

Tap the Zoom button to activate the feature, tap the zoom button again to deactivate it. If you want to try out this feature, go to a website and double-tap the screen with three fingers, the item on screen enlarges. Hold the screen with those three fingers and move the item around if you want. Double-tap with three fingers again to return to the default magnification.

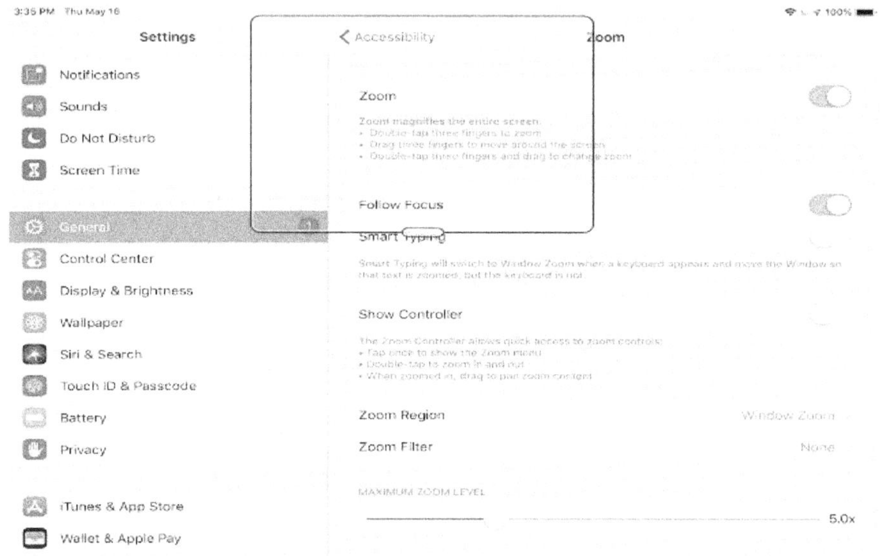

How to take night photos

You can utilize Night mode on your iPad to snap photos when the camera detects a dimly illuminated environment. Night mode is automatically brought in when the camera detects a low-light environment. The Night mode icon placed at the top of the camera screen is changed to yellow when the night mode feature is activated. Contingent upon how dark the environment is, night mode pictures might be taken quickly on your iPad or it might take a few seconds. Moreover, You can make certain alterations to your camera exposure setting. To obtain optimum results, hold your iPad steady until the object is captured, or position your iPhone on a solid and secure surface, or better still, use a tripod. To interrupt a Night mode photo mid-capture rather than holding on for the capture to be completed, simply tap the stop button beneath the slider.

Adjust the capture time

During the process of taking photos in Night mode, a number will be displayed near the Night mode icon to inform you how long the shot will take. To try longer Night mode photos, press the Night mode icon, afterwards use the slider above the shutter button to select Max, which prolongs the capture time. The moment you take the shot, the slider becomes a timer that counts down to the end of the capture time.

Taking Night mode selfies is pretty similar to taking normal selfies, simply open the Camera app and press the front-facing camera button and take the shot.

How to take square photos

Taking Square photos is a recent feature on Apple devices, it is particularly specific to Apple devices with iOS 14.

Taking square photos is pretty easy, go to the Camera application and press the ^ icon in the top mid portion of your screen, alternatively you can just swipe up on the viewfinder. An aspect ratio of 4:3 (that's the default) will be displayed, press it and select Square. Now, take your shots.

Auto low-light fps

In case you shoot videos with your iPhone in low-light environments, you may not always be provided with the results you hope for, this situation applies to shooting in 4K, 1080p, and 720p resolutions as well. However, a method which you can utilize to greatly improve your camera's video quality when shooting in a dim environment is the Auto low-light fps, you only need to make slight adjustments.

If you're snapping pictures with the Camera app, it automatically detects whether the scene is too dark, and Night mode will be brought in to optimize the image quality. However, this is not the case when it comes to shooting videos. To curb this, Apple has included a setting that when you activate it, it instantly decreases the fps rate in low-light environments to improve the quality of your video. To activate this feature, go to Settings, then "Camera," then to "Record Video." At this point, select the "Auto FPS" option, then apply the Auto FPS to the 30 fps video setting. You can even go further to switch these recording modes from inside the Camera app directly by pressing the frame rate at the edge. However, you have to be certain that the "Auto Low Light FPS" switch is enabled for each setting before you carry out the whole work from the Camera.

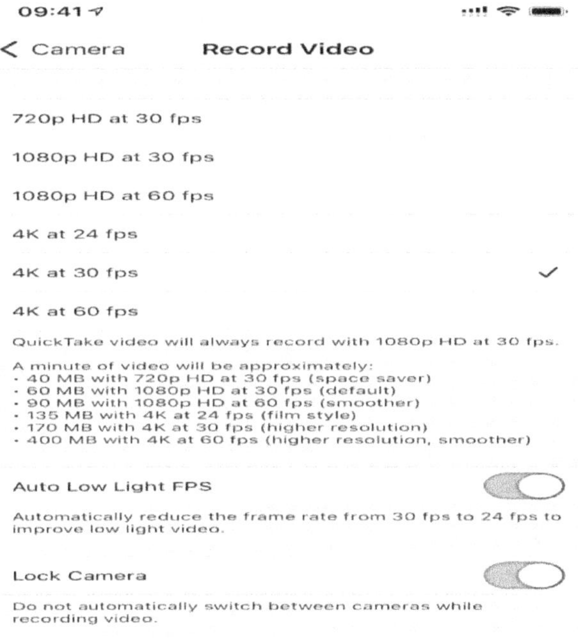

Only the 4K 30 fps, 1080p 30 fps, and 720p 30 fps are provided with the option.

This is how the auto-fps feature works; in the Camera application, anytime you're recording video and iOS finds out that the environment is not well illuminated, it will switch over to 24 fps. This switch can be done before you start recording the video or while you are recording if there's a sudden change in the intensity of illumination. This change in fps is almost unnoticeable as the indicator in the Camera app always displays your selected frame rate even if it plans on using 24 fps. Then the only way you can identify this fps change is through an EXIF analyser which informs you about the frame rate the video was shot with.

Chapter Four

How to customize text tones

Text tones aren't the only items you can customize on your iPad, you can go ahead to even come up with your personalized ringtones for phone calls, alarms, or anything you intend to. Text tones will be our focus here, and to customize it, we'll follow a step by step procedure;

- **Step 1: Include Your Sound File to iTunes**

Irrespective of whether you intend to utilize an abridged clip from a song for your tone or you have a favorite song you'd like to use instead, it is essential that you add the file to iTunes before starting. To implement this, hold the sound file on your iPad and drag and drop it over to your iTunes window. This automatically brings in the file, with that you can initiate the text tone process.

- **Step 2 : Put the time Parameters in place**

Text tones are originally designed to be as short as possible as most people do not want a lengthy ringtone alert playing every time a text is sent to them. Therefore, in case you intend to use a minor portion of a song as your text tone, you will most likely not want to upload the entire thing as a text tone. A useful help we that iTunes has provided us with here is that it allows users to set time parameters for songs, this grants users a sort of control over what portion of a song will be played.

After bringing in your song to iTunes, you can select by clicking the ellipsis (•••), or the "Edit" option in the menu bar, this displays the info page, then press "Options."

You will come cross the "start" and "stop" boxes. In these boxes, you can input the start time for your text tone and the end time. If your choice of selection differs from what the start or stop box offers, ensure the checkboxes are marked. The implication of this is that if the start box is left unchecked, the song will start at the beginning, and the stop box will let the song continue to the end, irrespective of the time you've imputed here.

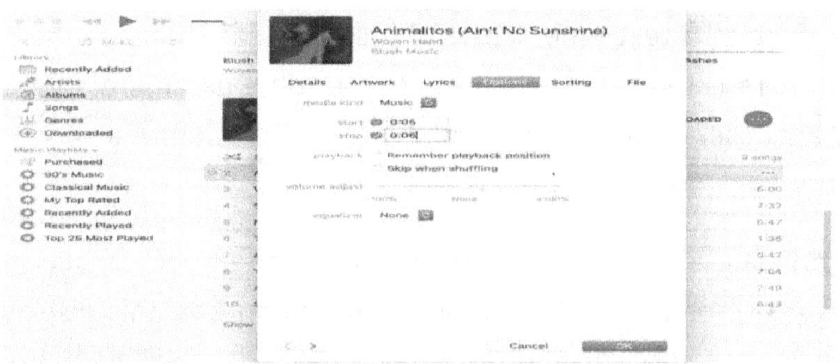

- **Step 3: Convert Your File to AAC**

In as much as your song or sound file is just the way you desire, there is a need to convert it to AAC, a file type with a higher-quality compression than MP3 but at the same bit rate. In essence, AAC is a better file type and the type a user needs in order to create a tone. However, converting your file to AAC isn't the only thing you'll be doing, you'll also be making a duplicate, hence you'll see two files in iTunes. If you're utilizing a song with time parameters, the duplicate you create will only be as long as your time limits. Rather than the full-length song, a new track listed at only one or two seconds will be displayed.

To do this conversion, press "File" on the menu bar, then "Convert." At this point, select "Create AAC Version." Your file will be converted, consequently giving rise to a new copy in AAC. In the event that "Create AAC Version" isn't displayed as an option for you, your conversion settings are likely to be different from what they need to be. To change the settings, go to "Preferences" in the menu bar, and select "Import Settings" in "General." Here, click "AAC Encoder" from the menu you will be provided with, press "Ok" to complete the process.

Another situation you might be faced with is when "Create AAC Version" is greyed-out, this implies that your song is DRM-protected and cannot be utilized as a text tone. Before concluding this step, ensure you go back to your original song file and reset the time parameters. Otherwise, what you'll basically hear is your text tone every time you try to play the full song.

- **Step 4: Convert your File Type from M4A to M4R**

Changing to AAC isn't enough for iOS to recognize your file as a tone. Your text tone, which is now seen as a .m4a file, has to be converted further to .m4r, a file type that is the standard for iOS tones.

To do this conversion, click the name of your file so it displays the name editor, then change its extension from .m4a or .m4r. While you're doing this, you can additionally change the name of the song to whatever you want your text tone to be called. Confirm the changes and proceed.

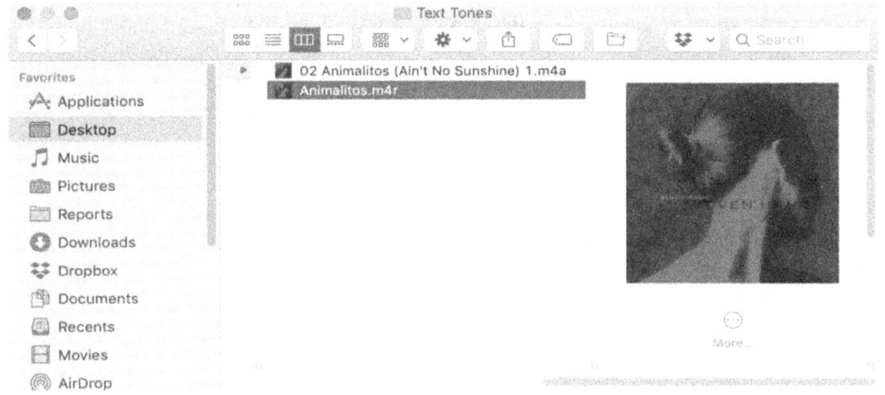

- **Step 5: Add the File to Tones**

You have to place your tone here. Press "Music" at the edge of the display, then click "Tones." If Tones isn't displayed, select "Edit Menu" then include it.

- **Step 6: Clean Up Your iTunes**

You might not want to leave behind the small mess you created just to set yourself up for text tones. Therefore, you can delete the duplicated abridged clip in the Music section, then go back to the original song and remove the start and stop times.

- **Step 7: Set Your Text Tone on Your iPhone or iPad**

If everything goes as it should, the text tone should be on your device now. Go to Settings –> Sounds (Sounds & Haptics on recent models) –> Text Tone. The issue here is, since you cannot identify custom ringtone from text tones, your tones will be listed under the Ringtones section at the bottom. Nevertheless, your custom sounds will appear above the stock ringtones. Furthermore, you can even assign this custom text tone to individual contacts. Open each contact page, press "Edit," select "Alert Tone," and choose your custom sound.

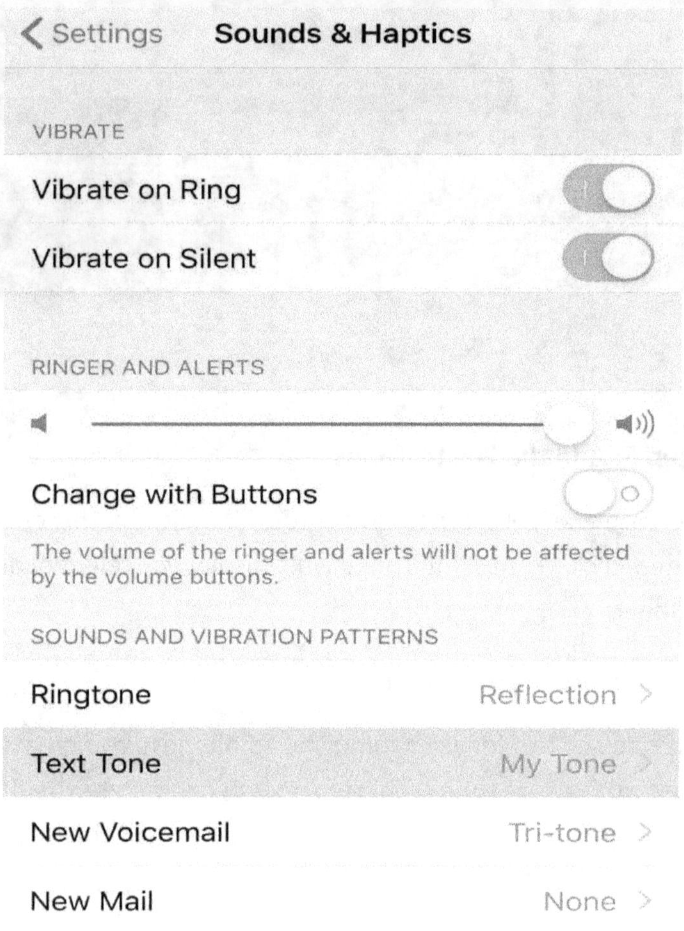

Turn on Dark Mode

There are a couple of ways to enable dark mode on your device:

- Activating dark mode on iPad with the brightness slider

This is basically the quickest method to enable dark mode. You simply Open Control Center on your iPad, then swipe down from the edge of your iPad. Next, press and hold the screen brightness slider and tap the Appearance button that will be displayed on the screen to switch between light and dark.

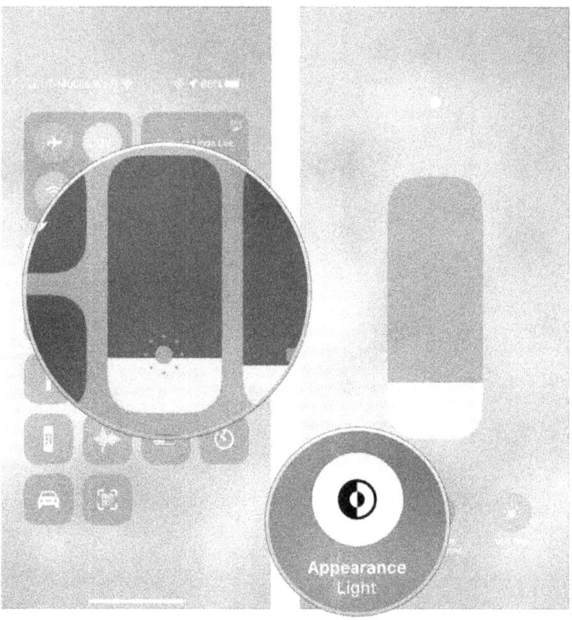

- **Setting up the Dark Mode toggle in Control Center**

Additionally, you can as well include a button specifically for Dark Mode to the Control Center on your iPad. With that in place, you can simply press the button to switch between Dark and Light modes. Simply go to settings on your iPad, press the Control Center, and then select Customize Controls.

At this point, press the + next to Dark Mode and drag on the handles to transform the buttons' position in the Control Center.

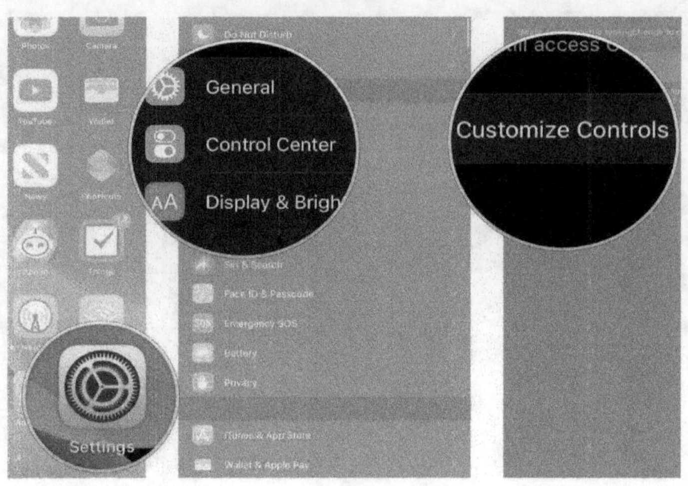

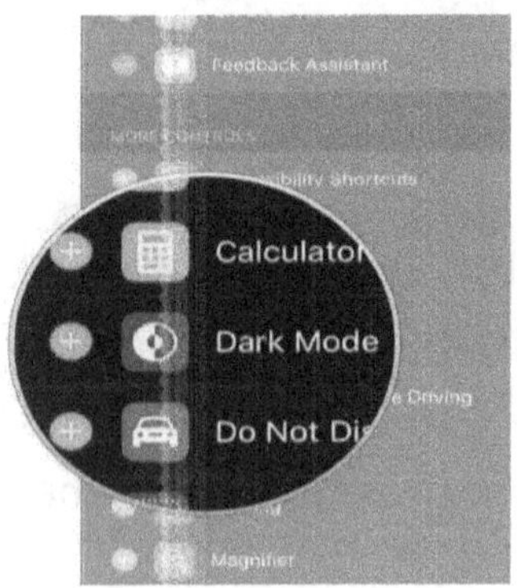

Activating dark mode on iPad with Settings

Go to settings on your iPad and press Display & Brightness. At this point, select either Light or Dark to choose which appearance to utilize.

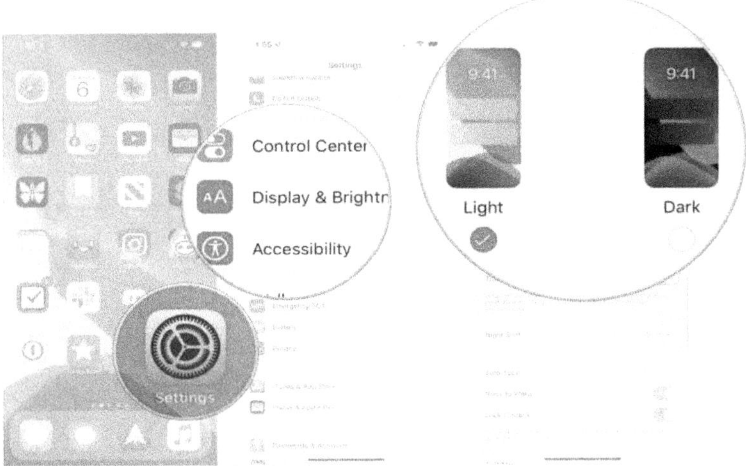

Now, press the switch close to Automatic so it is turned on, this makes your device to automatically transform between light and dark modes. Press Options, this displays the " Sunset to Sunrise", enabling this will make the dark mode activated from each sunset until the next sunrise.

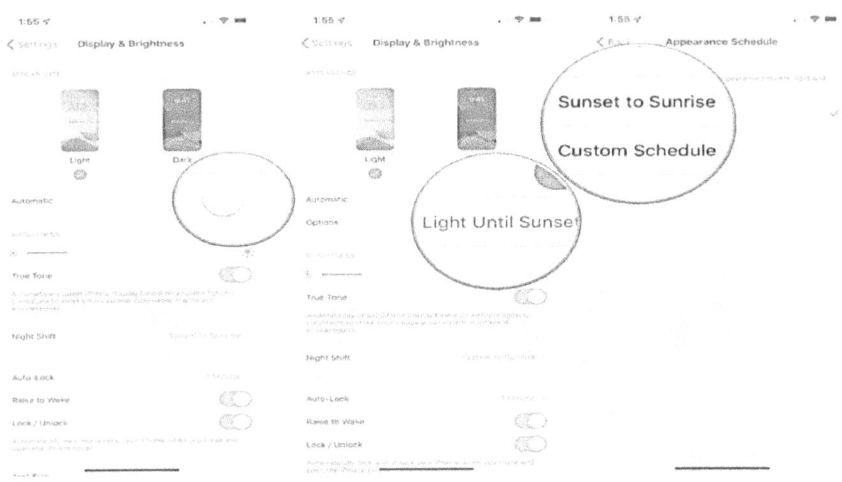

If you want to create your own custom schedule which creates a custom time range in which you want dark mode to be active, press "Custom Schedule". Press the light Appearance to determine when light mode should be activated, and the Dark Appearance to set when dark mode should be enabled.

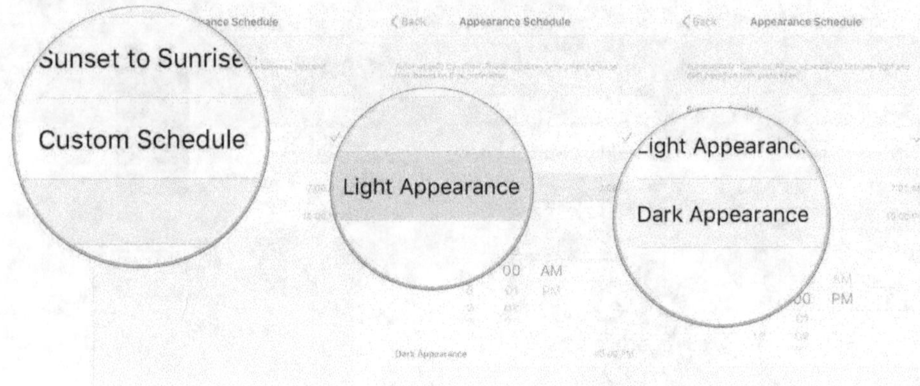

Set Wallpapers that react to dark mode

There are a number of default wallpapers on your device that react with your device's appearance settings. With these steps, you can also change the background wallpaper of your iPad to an Apple Dark Mode wallpaper.

Go to the Settings app on your device, then scroll down and press Wallpaper. Next, Choose a New Wallpaper, and tap Stills or Live; either of these options will provide you with the Dark Mode options.

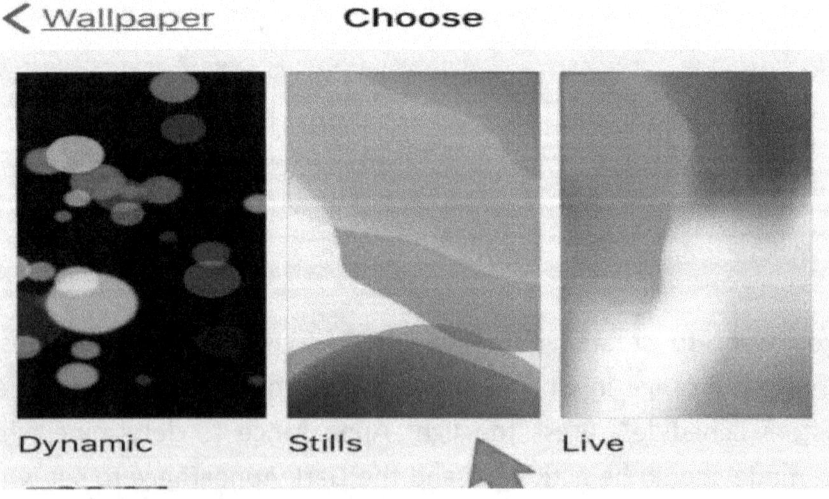

Select any of the wallpaper options displayed with the circular Dark Mode icon on it. Furthermore, you can retain the perspective zoom if you'd like the wallpaper to shift as the angle of your screen changes. You can disable the Perspective Zoom by pressing its icon and turning it off if you want your wallpaper to be static. In case this perspective zoom option isn't displayed, it's most likely because you've probably disabled the Reduce Motion option on your device. To enable the Reduce Motion feature, go to Settings > Accessibility > Motion and turn Reduce Motion off

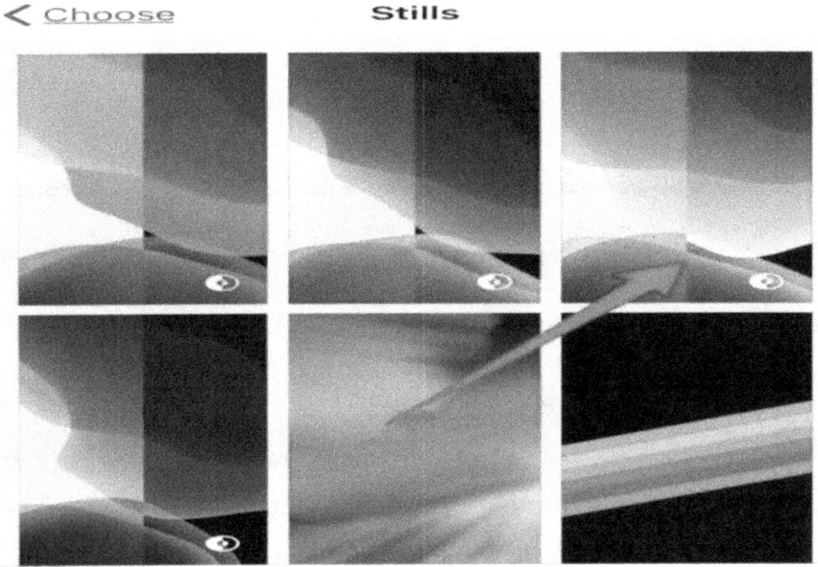

 Press Set to verify your wallpaper settings, or Cancel if you want to set a different Dark Mode wallpaper. Then press "Set Lock Screen, Set Home Screen, Set Both, or Cancel".

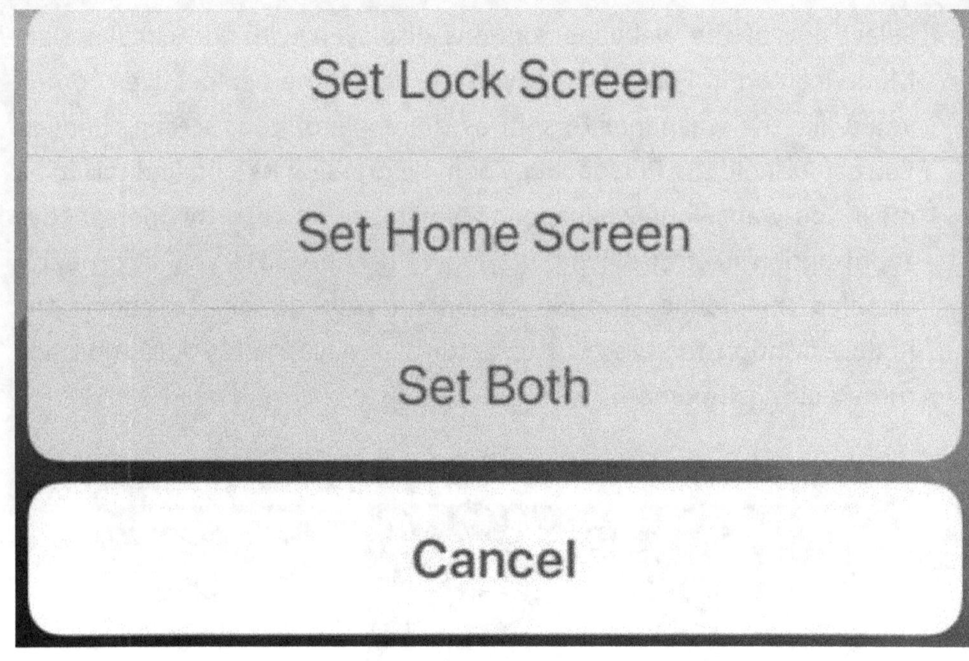

Setting Notification Preferences

You can make certain alterations to your notification settings.

- **How enable or disable notifications**

Perhaps you have this fear that you might miss out on important occasions or activities if you're not notified, and want to ensure you always know when something significant comes in on your iPhone or iPad, then you have to enable notifications. On the other hand, If you feel the Notification Center is becoming a mess and starting to piss you off, you can as well disable the unimportant ones from Notification Center.

Go to settings on your device and press Notifications.

Choose the application you intend to remove from Notification Center. You can then enable or disable the notifications from here.

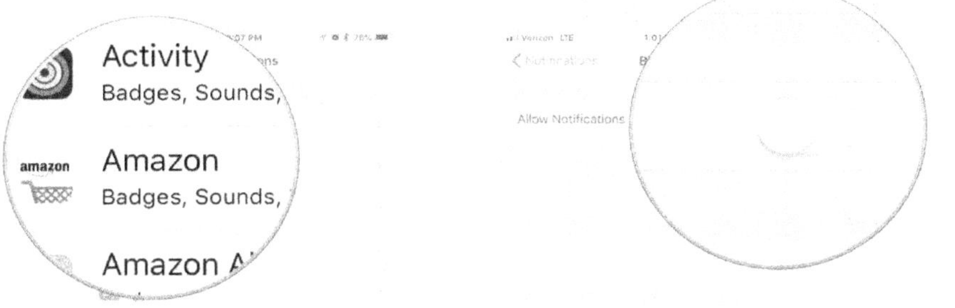

- **How to turn on or off Lock screen notifications on your iPhone and iPad**

Incase you don't want notifications from a number of apps to be shown on your Lock screen, here's how you can disable that:

Open the Settings app on your iPhone or iPad, then press Notifications. Now, choose the app for which you intend to have notifications appear on your Lock screen.

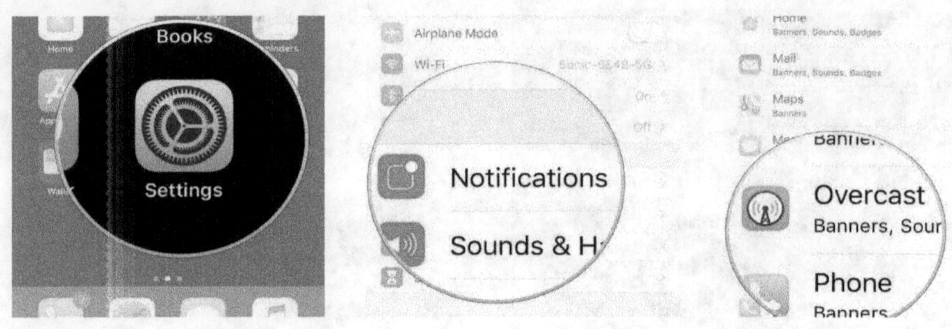

Press the Allow Notifications button to enable it if it's not already on, then press Lock Screen.

How to Set up text message forwarding

With this feature, the SMS/MMS messages that you sent to you or sent by your iPhone can be displayed on your Mac, iPad, and iPod touch. When an SMS or MMS message is sent to you on your iPhone/ iPad, it appears as a green bubble. iMessages are displayed as blue bubbles. With the Text Message Forwarding feature in place, you can send and receive the SMS and MMS messages from your iPhone on any Apple device touch that meets the Continuity system requirements.

Let's get into the set-up procedure, on your iPhone/ iPad, go to Settings > Messages > Send & Receive. Be certain that you're signed in to iMessage with the same Apple ID on all these devices.

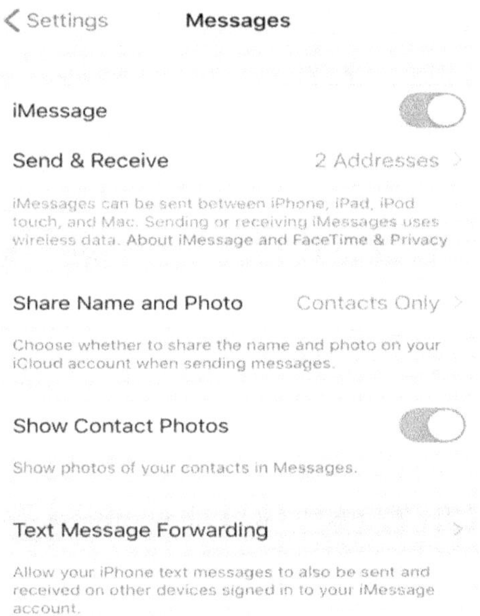

At this point, select which devices can send and receive text messages from your iPhone. If you didn't enable the two-factor authentication for your Apple ID, a verification code will be displayed in each of your other devices, input that code on your iPhone.

As long as your device is switched on and has an active internet connection, new SMS/MMS texts can be sent and received on the devices that are included.

When it comes to forwarding older text messages, simply touch and hold the message bubble that you intend to forward, and press More. Now, select any other text message to be forward, press the forward icon, enter a recipient and send.

Filter iMessage messages from unknown senders

Another useful feature on any Apple device is that in the Messages app , you can block disturbing messages, filter messages from unknown senders, and report spam messages. Filtering messages from senders you don't know, or senders you don't want, disables iMessage notifications from such senders. It then sorts the messages into the Unknown Senders tab in the Messages list. To do this, go to Settings > Messages. Here, you can enable or disable "Filter Unknown Senders".

How to enable iCloud Keychain on iPad

iCloud Keychain on your iPad enables you to create and store logins and passwords, credit card information, as well as other personal information across the entirety of your iPhone and iPad devices. iCloud Keychain can be utilized to access your stored information on your devices, however, it has to be enabled for you to use it.

Open the settings app on your iPad, and select your Apple ID banner. Then press iCloud.

Move down the page and select Keychain. Press the iCloud Keychain option to enable it, then input your Apple ID password if you're asked. In case you've initially set up an iCloud Keychain password, you will be asked to fill in your current password after enabling iCloud Keychain. If otherwise, you will need to come up with a new password.

Furthermore, this option has to be verified with another device. Nevertheless, when you decide to finalize your account, you'll then have to store important info more securely on your iPhone or iPad.

Deactivating iCloud Keychain on iPad

Peradventure you do not want iCloud Keychain to store your logins and passwords, credit card details, or personal information, it can be disabled.

Go to Settings on your iPhone or iPad, and press your Apple ID banner. Then, Tap iCloud. Move down the page and select Keychain. Tap the iCloud Keychain to disable it. If at any point you're asked whether you want to disable Safari AutoFill feature, select "Delete from my iPad" to be stored only in iCloud, or "Keep on my iPad" so the data is stored on your iPad. Insert your Apple ID password where necessary.

How to activate Siri

- **How to use Siri**

Press the home button on your iPad for a few seconds, or simply say "Hey, Siri", this activates Siri and you can start stating your command or question.

- **How to edit a Siri question or command**

Incase Siri didn't hear you clearly, or there is a mistake, or perhaps you changed your mind, you can easily change the question or command by pressing the microphone icon and asking Siri the question or state the command again.

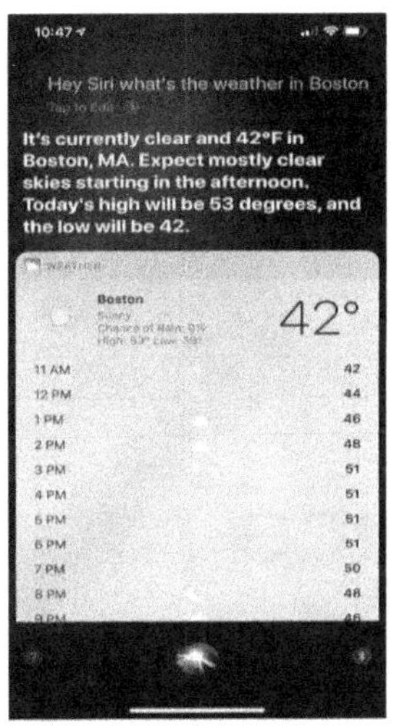
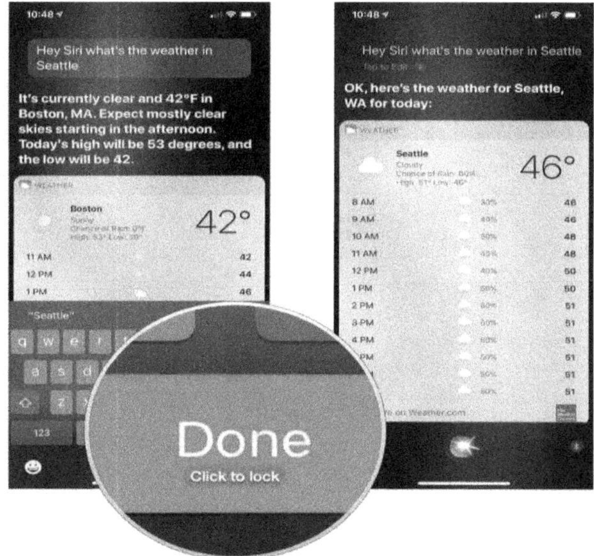

Alternatively, if you want to edit a request you initially made, you can just tap edit to edit it. Input your changes and then press Done on the bottom right of the keyboard.

- How to enable and disable Siri in the Settings app

You will be inquired by iOS if you intend to enable Siri when you first set up your iPad. Incase Siri isn't already activated, you can always enable it in Settings. The same procedure applies when you want to disable it. To do this, go to settings on your iPad.

Move down the page and press Siri & Search. Press the switch that is placed near "Listen" to enable Hey Siri. Afterwards, press the switch near Home, this enables Sri to permit the Home button access to Siri. Press the switch that is placed next to" Allow Siri When Locked" so you can activate Siri when your device is locked.

- Changing Siri's language

Open Settings from your Home screen, then press Siri & Search. Afterwards, press Language, then select a language.

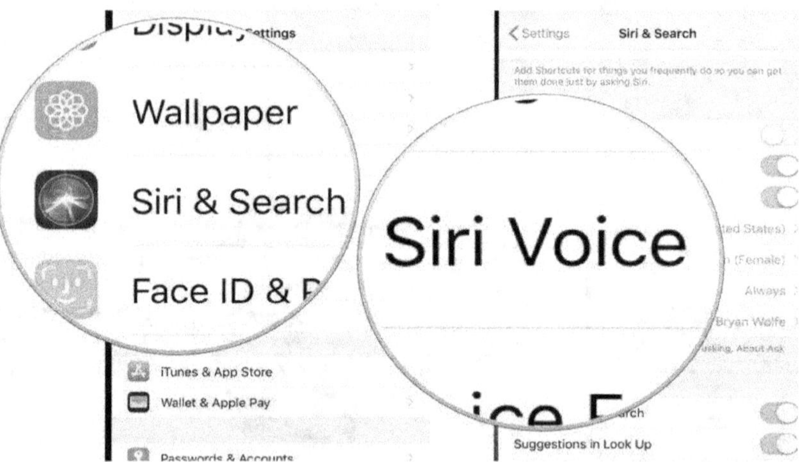

Chapter Five

How to set your language on your iPad

Numerous language options are provided on the iPad and you can switch from one language to another. All you have to do is open the Settings app from the home screen and select General. Then, press Language & Region.

At this point, press iPad Language at the crest of the screen. Next thing is to select the language you would like to switch to, after that, press Done

How to Scan Documents in the Files App

If there is a need to scan a document or file, you can also utilize your iPad to do that. There are numerous apps and options that can be utilized to scan files to your mobile device, however a relatively easier way to do this is to utilize the built-in Files app. A document can be scanned by taking a picture of it with your device and afterwards saving it to any of your online storage sites or other locations set up through the Files app.

Most importantly, your iPad must be running on iPadOS 13.1 or higher, the iPad Air runs on iPadOS 14, so we have nothing to worry about. Next, launch the Files app on your device, through this app, you can create an interface with online services such as OneDrive and Google

Drive, network servers and NAS devices, and other locations. Files that you store in these locations can then be accessed. If these online services are already in place, and then you're good to go. While you're in the Files app, tap the ellipsis icon(•••) placed at the crest of the Browse pane and choose the command to Scan Documents.

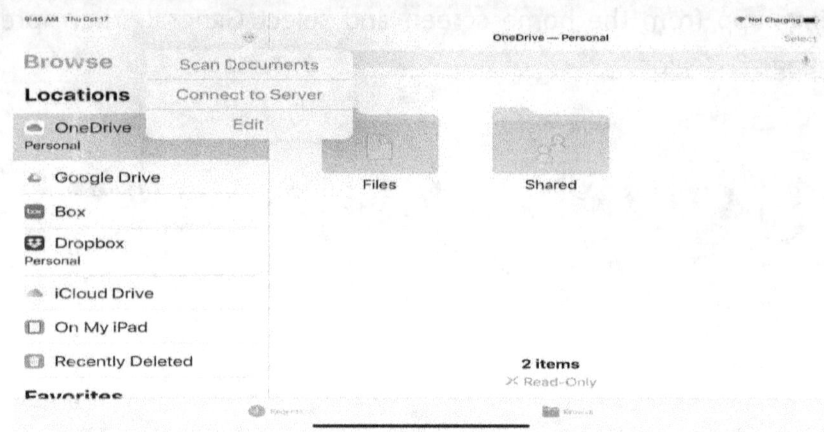

Now, place the document you intend to scan on a flat surface, ensure it's within the framing of your device's camera. Meanwhile, on the iPad's camera, hold on until the area you intend to scan has a blur highlight displayed on it. You can then enable the Auto option, what this does is to cause the camera to automatically capture the scan when the document is properly assembled. As an alternative, this option can changed to Manual, this implies that you need to press the shutter button on your device take the scan

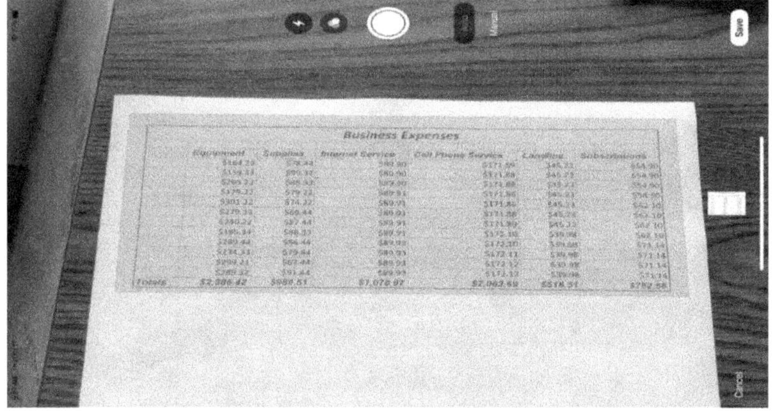

After you've taken the scan, you may come across an inquiry page asking whether you want to crop the image. If you want to crop, you can do so by dragging the handles at the corners of the scan. Furthermore, you can also choose the option to Retake the scan if you're not satisfied with the outcome of the initial scan.

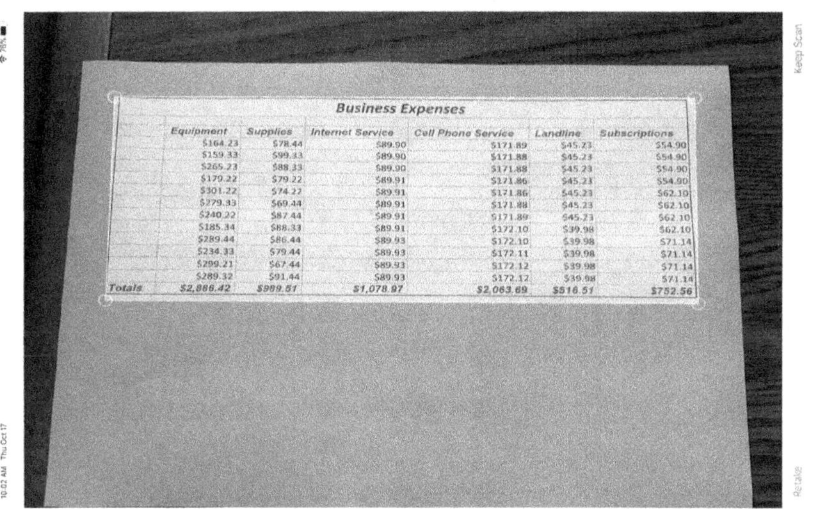

Business Expenses

	Equipment	Supplies	Internet Service	Cell Phone Service	Landline	Subscriptions
	$164.23	$78.44	$89.90	$171.89	$45.23	$54.90
	$159.33	$99.33	$89.90	$171.88	$45.23	$54.90
	$265.23	$88.33	$89.90	$171.88	$45.23	$54.90
	$170.22	$79.22	$89.91	$171.86	$45.23	$54.90
	$301.22	$74.22	$89.91	$171.86	$45.23	$62.10
	$279.33	$69.44	$89.91	$171.88	$45.23	$62.10
	$240.22	$87.44	$89.91	$171.89	$45.23	$62.10
	$185.34	$88.33	$89.91	$172.10	$39.98	$62.10
	$289.44	$86.44	$89.93	$172.10	$39.98	$71.14
	$234.33	$79.44	$89.93	$172.11	$39.98	$71.14
	$299.21	$67.44	$89.93	$172.12	$39.98	$71.14
	$289.32	$91.44	$89.93	$172.12	$39.98	$71.14
Totals	$2,886.42	$989.51	$1,078.97	$2,063.69	$516.51	$752.56

On the next screen that will be displayed, press the button to Save your scanned image, after which you press the "Name Scanned Document" to change the name of the scanned image. Then press Done

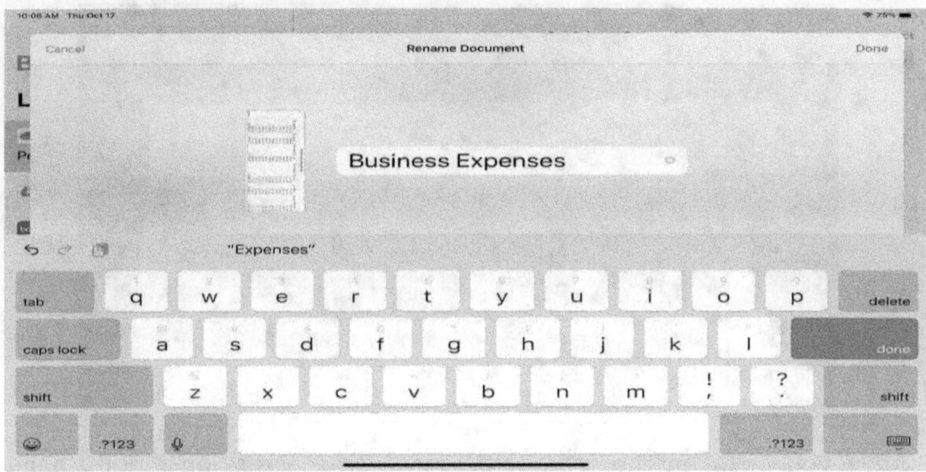

At this point, select the location where you want your scan to be saved on your device. Contingent upon which services and locations you've put in place in the Files app, you can opt to save the file on OneDrive, Google Drive, Box, Dropbox, iCloud Drive, on your iPhone or iPad, or on a network drive or NAS. Select any location that suits you, and press Save.

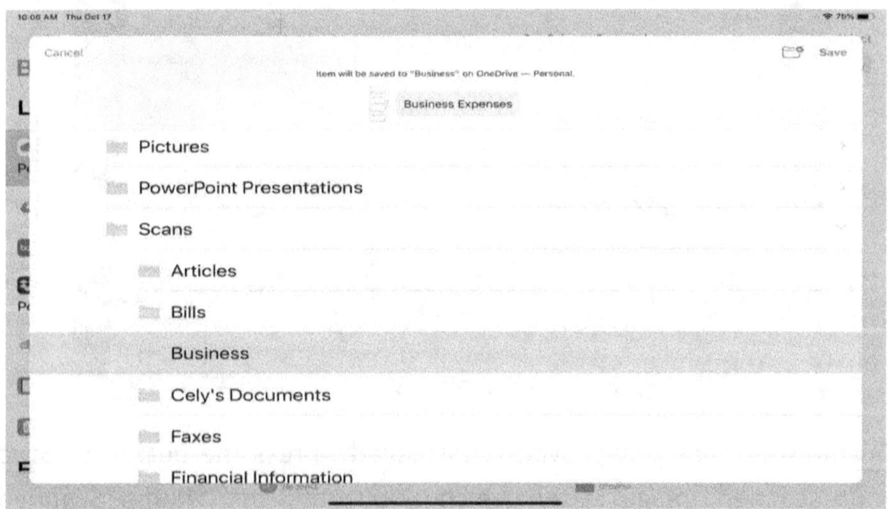

Share Pictures without Location Information

Basically, every picture you take on your device has a number of information attached to it, one of which is the Location where you took the picture. Location Information about a picture is useful when it comes to creating memories, organizing pictures into albums, and so on. However, if you feel it's a breach on your privacy for your pictures to show your location when you share such pictures, then you can disable the "Location Information" option.

This is what you need to do; open the photos app on your device and select a photo. Then press the share button on the photo and select "Options" at the top. Afterwards, go to the Include section, you'll see the Location option, press this option so as to disable it. What this does is that it removes the location data when you share the picture, however, the location details will still be retained on your device.

How to remove app size limitations on cellular data

Another significant change Apple has included right from the arrival of iOS 13 is to enable users to download apps over cellular irrespective of their size. During iOS 12, users were restricted to download apps that are not more than 200MB when using cellular data, initially the limit was 150MB and was later changed to 200MB as an improvement, nevertheless, it still wasn't ideal. However, with iOS 13's and higher iOS, there is no limit. Now, users are provided with the option of choosing whether to place that restriction themselves or not. Here's how to go about it so you can download any app over cellular data, not minding its size.

Go to Settings on your device and press the iTunes & App Store option, just below the Cellular Data field, select App Downloads. At this point, select the Always Allow option. And that is all, now you can download stuff on your device with your cellular data irrespective of the size.

How to take long screenshot of websites

Open your Safari browser and load any website of your choice that you intend to take a screenshot of on your iPhone or iPad. Now, take a screenshot utilizing the Volume Up + Side Button combination, or the screenshot combination that is functional for your device.

Afterwards, a small preview will be displayed at the bottom corner of the screen, press this preview. Pressing the preview will direct you to the familiar screenshot annotation and markup view. You'll notice a recent tab positioned at the top. At this point, tap on Full Page. Without any delay, you'll see that the entire web page preview is displayed on the screen. The scroll bar on the right can be utilized to go through this full page. Likewise, you can make use of any tool to label the screenshot. At this point, you can press the Done button so you'll be provided with the option of saving to files, and then you select a folder on your iPhone/iPad or on iCloud Drive. Moreover, you can equally press the Share button so that the screenshot is sent as a mail attachment.

As soon as the storage location is confirmed, iOS will save the screenshot as a PDF which you can access in the Files app, and share with any app of your choice.

How to customize how notifications are grouped

Definitely, you can make a bit of adjustments to your notification center, how it looks and operates. Notifications are grouped into batches, this makes addressing them to be much more easier. Nevertheless, you can customize how notifications are grouped.

Go to settings on your iPhone or iPad, and select Notifications. Then pick the application you intend to customize its notification grouping.

Next, press Notification Grouping. If you want suggestions as to how your app notifications should be grouped from Siri, press "Automatically". At this point, press By App so that the notifications will be grouped by app. However, if you want to disable the notification grouping feature, press "Off"

How to manage notifications from Notification Center

In the same manner, notifications can be managed and attended to in the Notification Center. The application, which the notification relates to can be opened by swiping to the right on that notification. Meanwhile, swiping to the left on the notification enables you to manage, view, or clear the notification. Here's how to go about it:

Unlock your device and swipe down from the crest of your screen to bring in the Notification Center. Swipe towards the left on a Notification to display your options.

If you want the entire notifications to be removed from the stack, press Clear All. However, if you want to open the applications related to that notification, press View, or just press Manage to swiftly carry out an action on an app's notifications.

Furthermore, you can just select Deliver Quietly to bring in certain adjustments to the settings for the notification. What this "Deliver Quietly" option does is that it allows notifications to show up in Notification Center, but it will not be displayed on the Lock screen, neither will it play a sound, show a banner, nor display a badge on the app icon.

Press Turn Off if you want the notifications for that app to be disabled altogether, or press Settings to customize the app's notifications in the Settings app.

How to Switch Apps

In the recent versions of iPadOS, Slide Over for iPad permits numerous apps to be in the Slide Over mode, this is more or less an active iPhone application on the side of the iPad screen. Similarly, users can likewise switch between apps that are in Slide Over on the iPad. Switching between apps in Slide Over tends to increase the productivity of the users when they're really conversant with how it works.

1. Remember we earlier stated that Slide Over a sort of an iPhone app positioned at the edge of your iPad's display? Yes, that's

exactly how it is and switching apps in Slide Over in a similar manner as it is on a modern iPhone. For iPad, here's how this feature operates; Bring in the Slide Over mode on iPad with two or more different apps. Then swipe the navigation bar placed at the base of the window to scroll through the apps you have just used.

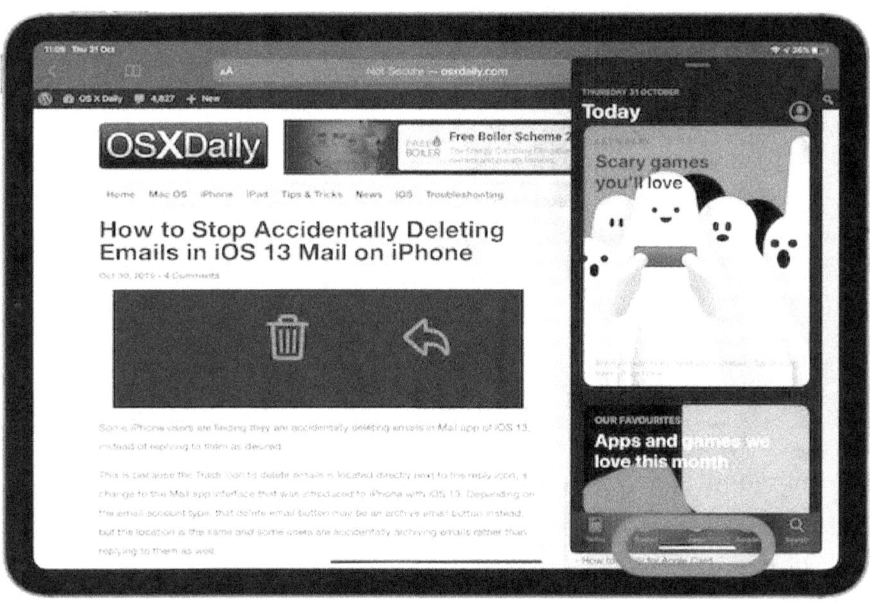

The moment you get to the application you intend to work on, stop swiping. The thing is If you happen to be an iPad user with an iPhone experience, you'll observe the similarity to iPhone multitasking. A whole card-based display of your recently used apps is what you will see. You can just swipe through to slide over applications just the same way it is done on the iPhone

Bring in numerous apps to the Slide Over view on iPad, then swipe up from the navigation bar and hold your position at the mid-portion of the window for a moment. As soon as the multitasking view is displayed, take off your finger and swipe to select the app you intend to use.

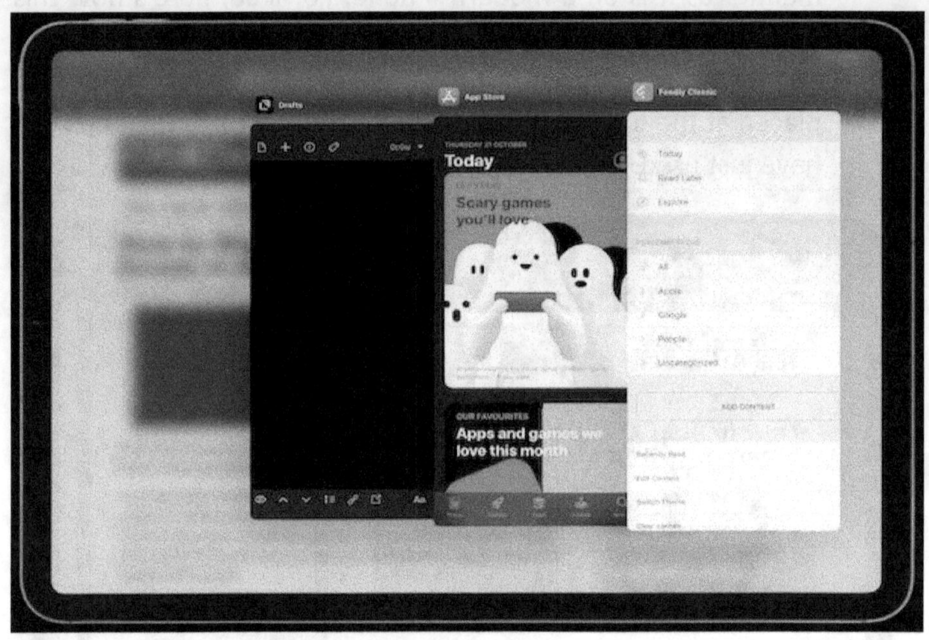

This upgraded Slide Over multitasking included in the latest iPadOS versions really does have the potential to be very helpful particularly for those who carry out daily activities on iPad.

How to force quit an app on iPad

Let's say there are a couple of applications running in your background and you want to close them so as to save battery or any other reason, you can force quit the application. Double-click on your iPad's Home button, and locate the application you intend to removein the app switcher. When you locate the app, swipe up on it and that's all, you've just force quit the application.

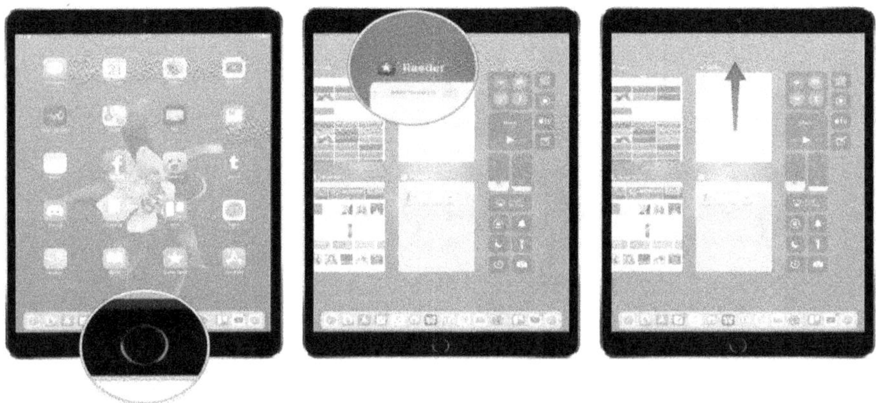

How to force quit an app on the iPad using a gesture

Likewise, you can utilize a gesture to help you force quit an application on your iPad. This is how to go about it; whileyou are in that application, swipe up from the base of the screen with just one finger. This brings in the dock, swipe up again so it takes you to the application-switching interface and Control Center.

Locate the application you intend to quit in the app switcher. Afterwards, swipe up on that application that you intend to force quit.

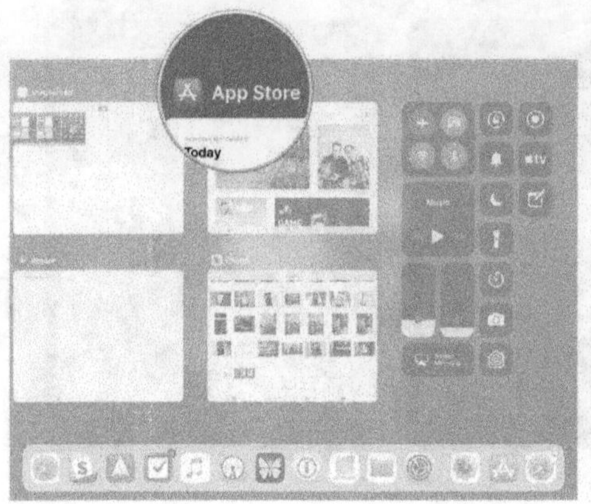

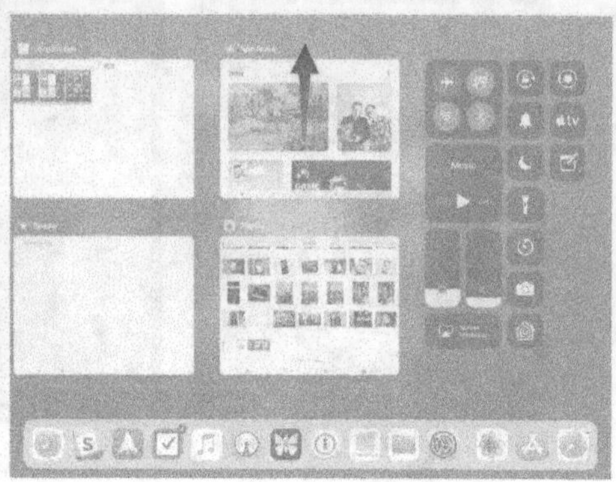

And that is all. Additionally, there is an extra option for initiating the force quitting process, and you can also enter the Control Center during this process if need be.

How to Access Readability Mode

Readability Mode can be activated in order to enhance the reading habits of the user. When you're active on a website that supports Reader View on your iPhone or iPad, the address bar located at the crest of the screen will state "Reader View Available" when you initially get into the site. In case it doesn't state this, it implies that it cannot be used on that particular site.

Go to Safari from your Home screen and load the website you'd like to peruse. After that, press the Reader button on the left of the address bar. It resembles a series of stacked lines.

With that, Reader View has been activated. Something you'll notice is that much of the color and animations will be erased and only a simple screen of text will be displayed.

When the need to disable Reader View comes up, simply press the Reader button again.

Share Music over AirPods

You can as well share music on your AirPods, to your iOS device or to another person with an iOS device. First, interface your AirPods to your iOS device. Then press the AirPlay icon in the Control Center or the Lock screen or in the app you're listening to. At this point, press Share Audio. Peradventure your friend has AirPods too, bring them near your device with the AirPods embedded in the case and with the lid opened. The moment your friend's AirPods shows up on your screen, tap Share Audio.

When you want to stop sharing, press the AirPlay icon in the Control Center, then press the checkmark next to the headphones you intend to stop sharing with. The moment you stop sharing audio, the second set of AirPods are also disconnected.

Chapter Six

Set up Monthly Cycle Data

You can set up your monthly cycle data by utilizing the Health app on your iPad/iPhone. To begin tracking your monthly cycle, just a few changes need to be made in the Health app. Go to the Health app on your device and press the Browse tab. After that, press Cycle Tracking.

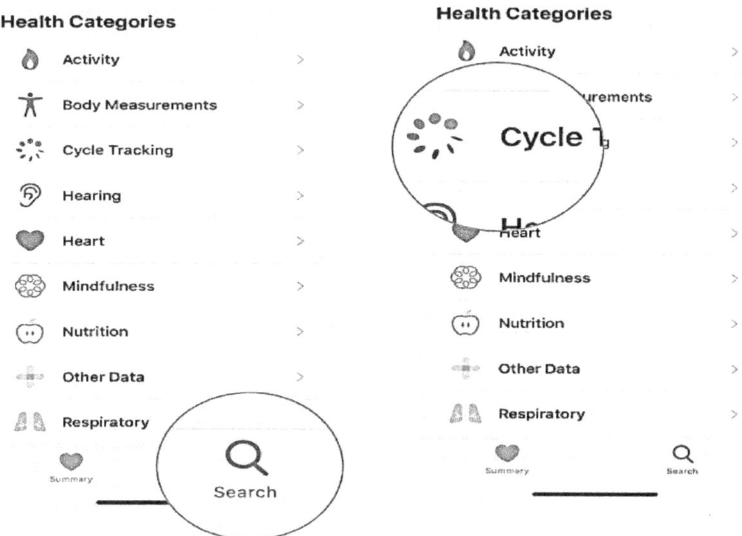

A number of options will be displayed above the Cycle Log, press these options and move down the page. Here, press Period Length and input your period length. Next is the Cycle length stage, tap this option and fill in the average number of days you have between successive periods.

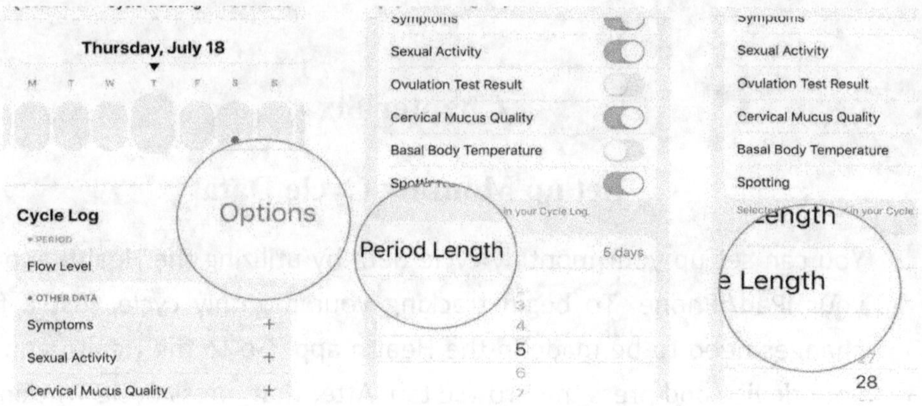

With this details you've provided, the Health app comes up with a prediction and fertility calendar based on when your period actually starts

How to customize your Cycle Tracking options in the Health app on iPhone

You can make selections as regards the aspects of your cycle you intend to log every day, week, and month. For instance, probably you're trying to conceive, it is advisable to include the entire cycle log options. In case you decide to keep track of when you're supposed to have your menstrual period again, the entire cycle logging options can be left off. Here's where you can locate them.

Open the Health app on your device, then go to the Browse tab and press Cycle Tracking.

Afterwards, select Options that's at the top of the Cycle Log. Press the Symptoms switch so it displays the selected symptoms in your Health app log. These symptoms include;

Abdominal cramps

Acne

Appetite Changes

Bloating

Breast tenderness

Constipation

Diarrhoea

Headache

Hot Flashes

Lower back pain

Mood changes

Nausea

Ovulation Pain

Tiredness

Sleep changes

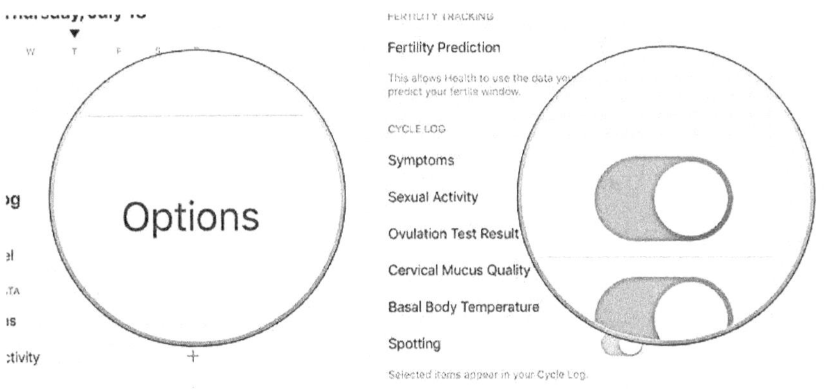

You can press Options, and then enable Symptoms. Move to the Sexual Activity aspect and press the switch, this enables it so it displays your logged sexual activity. In a similar fashion, enable the Ovulation Test Results so you are shown the ovulation test results you have logged in. Follow this pattern and enable the options for Cervical Mucus Quality, Basal Body Temperature, and spotting.

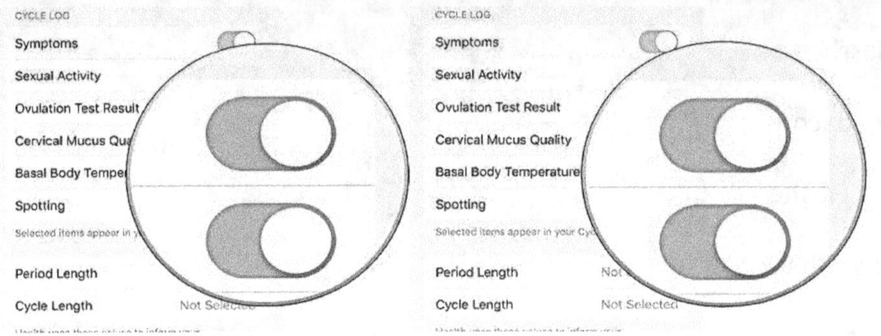

How to set up fertility predictions and notifications in the Health app on iPhone

Perhaps you're directing your efforts at conceiving, the fertility tracker will be of help here too by pinpointing your most fertile days in each month. This is contingent upon the manual information you filled in when you initially started your period and any ovulation tests that were logged in by you. Your fertility prediction calendar functions based on the activities that occur three weeks before or after your period.

Open the Health app on your device and move to the Browse tab. Here, select Cycle Tracking. Press Options positioned at the top of the Cycle Log. Press the Fertility Prediction switch to activate it, this enables it to come up with a three-week calendar of your coming fertility window. The press the fertility Notification switch to activate it, this informs you about your next likely fertility window.

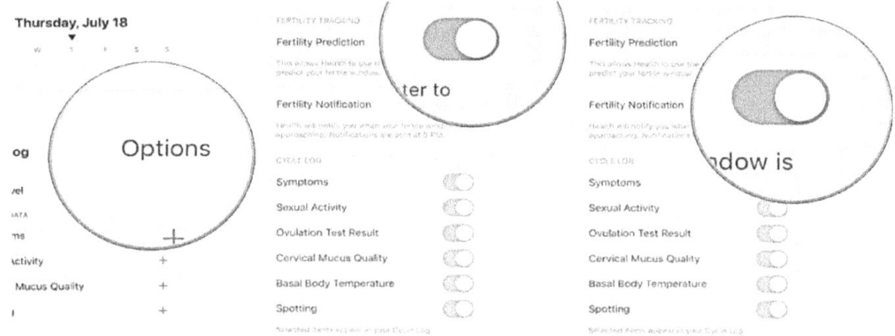

How to set up period predictions and notifications in Cycle Tracking

One of the very handy features of Cycle Tracking is period predictions. This employs the details you inputted manually about the usual duration of your period coupled with your average monthly cycle, that is the interval between successive periods. Initially, when you fill in the first day of your period, a two-month out calendar is crafted to show you a prediction of when you should expect the two coming periods to fall into. Furthermore, you can enable notifications to notify you when you're about a week away from these estimated dates and remind you to log your data.

Open the Health app on your device and move to the Browse tab. Here, select Cycle Tracking. Press Options positioned at the top of the Cycle Log.

Press the Period Prediction switch to enable this option, this crafts out a two-month period prediction calendar. Then, press the Period Notification switch to enable it, this ensures you receive alerts about your upcoming period and reminders to log your daily data.

How to log a cycle symptom to Cycle Tracking in the Health app on ipad Air

Regardless of whether you're actively on your period at the moment, or you just intend to log significant information relating to your cycle, be it symptoms relating to your pre or post-menstrual days, this can be done at any time in the Health app.

Open the Health app on your device and move to the Browse tab. Here, select Cycle Tracking. Press Symptoms, and fill in the entire symptoms that you have experienced from the list and press Done.

Moving to the aspect that states "Other Data" in Cycle Tracker, you can as well include data relating to your cervical mucus viscosity, the day's sexual activity, and whether or not you've discovered any spotting.

How to log a cycle symptom to Cycle Tracking on Apple Watch

Similar to logging your period, you can likewise log your cycle symptoms every day, right on your Apple Watch.

Press the Digital Crown present on your Apple Watch to bring in the app tray, afterwards press the Cycle Tracking app and select Symptoms. At this point, select the entire related symptoms you've experienced from the list, then press Done

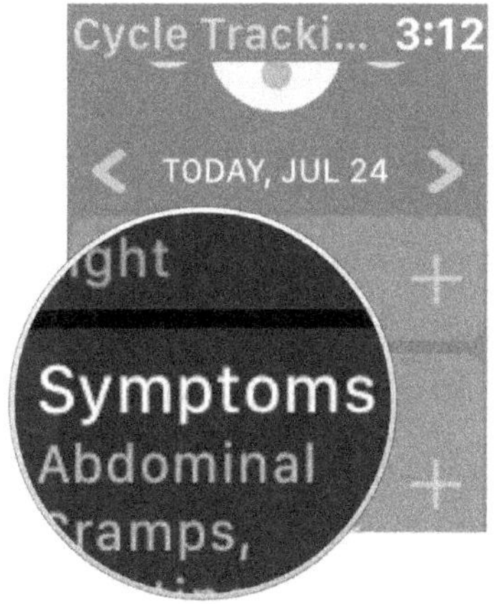

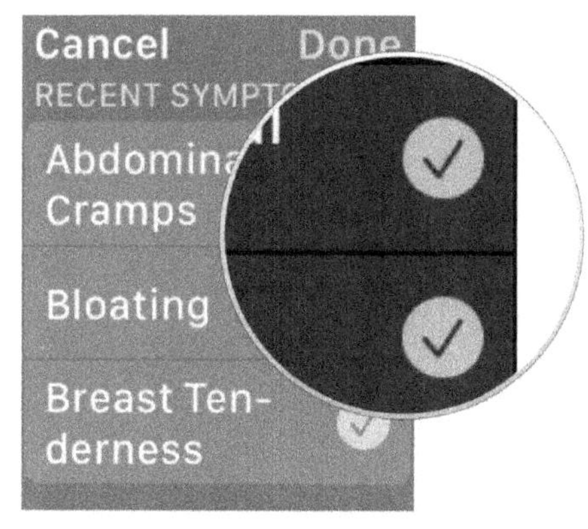

Right from your Apple Watch, you can as well include data relating to your cervical mucus viscosity, the day's sexual activity, and whether or not you've discovered any spotting.

How to delete Cycle Tracking Data in the Health app

Deleting the data you've logged in to the health app isn't so arduous to figure out. If by chance, there is an error in any of the activities you have logged in, and you want to delete the data entirely, just adhere to these steps to get it done.

Open the Health app on your device and move to the Browse tab. Here, select Cycle Tracking. Move to the base of the Cycle Tracking summary and press View Cycle Tracking Item. At this point, select the Category Log you intend to erase. Here, move down the page and select Show All Data.

 In the page displayed to you, press Edit at the edge of the screen. After that, press the Remove button placed close to the data you intend to erase. It resembles a red dot bearing a minus symbol inside. Then, press Delete and that is all.

Chapter Seven

Disable True Tone

Devices built with True Tone technology entail sensors that estimate the ambient light color and brightness. The device then employs these details to automatically alter its display, therefore it can make corrections to white point and illumination depending on your surrounding lighting so as to provide you with the appropriate sorts of white regardless of the conditions. This feature isn't new as numerous desktop monitors have been embedded with for quite some time. The item to note is that the human optical system is constantly making comparisons with near-white to an item that's entirely white and that white appears to be perfect seem to influence our the contrast we are familiar with at whatever we're looking at, this implies that a white point you've adjusted should be more pleasing to our eyes.

Furthermore, it connotes that devices with True Tone should appear to be more readable in direct sunlight, thereby improving their usability. Another significant component here for creatives, which ensures that the colours that are displayed maintain their accuracy and consistency.

By default, True Tone has been enabled;however, it can be activated or deactivated. To do this, simply adhere to this step: On iPhone and iPad, go to Settings > Display & Brightness > press the True Tone button to activate or deactivate it.

There are numerous reasons why you should disable True Tone, one is Personal preference such as Night Shift or auto-brightness. At certain times, all you desire is for the screen to remain static and not changing while you're glancing at it.

How to Apply Filter to Videos

Pictures aren't the only item you can add filters to on your device, you can as well add filters to videos just to improve its aesthetics and do whatever pleases you to it. To do this, go to the Photos app on your device and be certain that the video you intend to apply a filter to has been selected and it is active on the screen. After that, press the "Edit" button. Next, press the Filters icon, the filter icon resembles a minute venn diagram just as shown in the image.

You will be provided with nine different filters to make your selections from. Go through these filters to select the one you intend to use. Moreover, a preview of each filter will be exhibited so you can be precise about your decision. A new slider will be displayed just beside the filter. Slide it to make changes to the manner in which the dramatic the applied filter will be. Similarly, a preview of this will be displayed just to ensure you make selections that's appropriate for the content you're editing. Afterwards, press "Done" when you're okay with the selection.

These alterations you've made to the video will be effected, and the video will be saved. Nevertheless, this might take a few seconds contingent upon the duration of the video and the device you're utilizing. Interestingly, any changes you include will also be synchronized via iCloud if you're utilizing iCloud Photo Library.

How to edit Videos

How to Trim Videos on an iPad

Trimming a video is among the very basic editing activities you can carry out on your device. Just like the way you can trim prior to sharing in certain applications, you can as well do this in the Photos app.

Adhere to these steps to trim your video:

After opening your photos app, go to the video you intend to trim. Then, press "Edit" in the bottom edge of that video. At this point, a Play button and the video's timeline should be evident. Utilize the arrow placed on the left side to change the video's start point, while the arrow that you see on the right side can be utilized to change the video's endpoint.

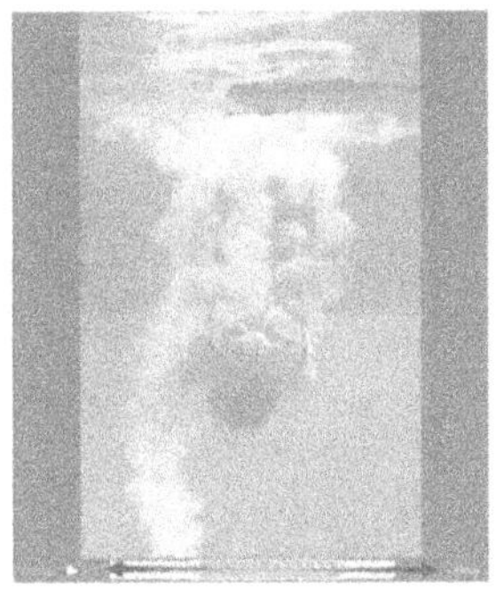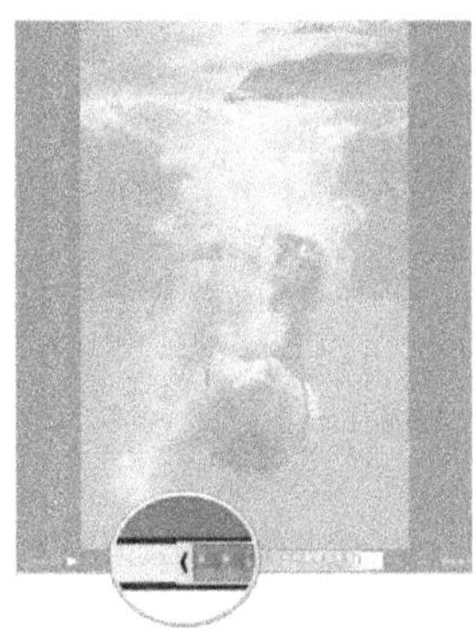

Next, press the Play button in order to show the preview of the editing you've made. If you're satisfied with these changes, press "Done," and then pick "Save Video" or "Save Video as New Clip" to create a duplicate of that video.

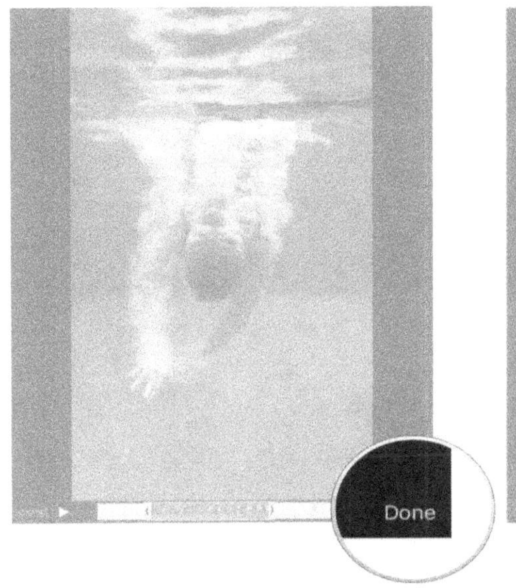

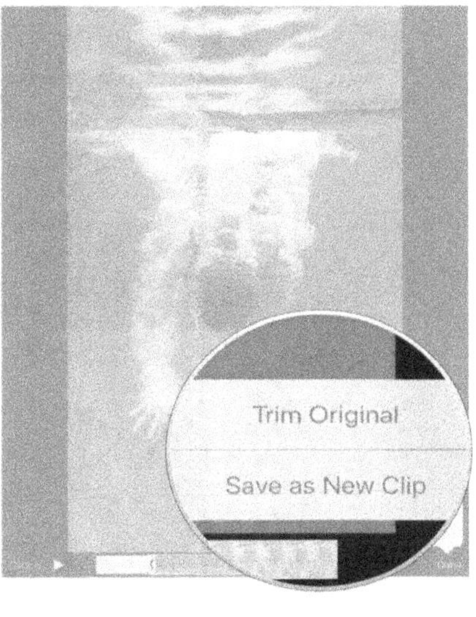

Additionally, editing in iOS isn't the destructive type, this implies that if you choose "Save Video," no footage of the video will be lost. At any point in time, you can always re-edit the video to bring in the footage you trimmed.

- **How to Rotate Videos on an iPad**

Adhere to these steps on how to rotate a video:

After opening your photos app, go to the video you intend to change its aspect ratio or rotate, and press "Edit" at the bottom edge of that video. Afterwards, press the Rotate/Crop icon placed at the base of the screen.

Now, at the top edge of that screen, press the Rotate 90 degrees icon (the box that has an arrow on top of it). Keep on pressing the button repeatedly until you get to an appropriate aspect ratio. Then, press "Done" to include your changes.

How to Merge Videos on an iPad

For this particular task, we'll need to bring in a third-party app that merges videos. Interestingly, Apple offers iMovie for free, which eases the work needed to merge two or more videos.

Download the iMovie app on your iPhone or iPad, this is a free app so you have nothing to worry about. After downloading it, open the application and you'll come across the "Projects" screen. Press the plus sign (+) to initiate a new project, and after that, press "Movie" when necessary. At this point, you are meant to select the videos you intend to merge, although you can later include any other videos you want to merge. Next, move the edges of each video to trim clips directly in this screen.

After selecting the clips, press "Create Movie" at the base of the screen. What you will then see is your selected clips placed on a video timeline one by one. To trim these videos, select the videos by tapping it, then hold the edges of each frame, and then move them to the points of your choice.

How to Adjust Video Exposure, Contrast and More

Adjustments can also be made to various image parameters on videos in a similar fashion with photos. Users of iPad Air 4 are granted access to a complete gamut of editing tools, including automatic enhancement. These changes are not hard and fast, hence they can be undone at a later time if you wish. In your photos application, choose the video you intend to edit, and press "Edit" in the video's displayed screen. Next, press the Adjustments icon at the base of the screen, and go through the numerous image features, and change the position of the slider to adjust the image. When you're satisfied with these edits, press done "Done."

The most ideal method you can utilize to learn the functions of each of these settings is by playing around, exploring and experimenting with them.

How to Revert a Video to Its Original State

To revert means to return or "Convert backwards" to an initial or previous state. Any video or photo with filters or edits can be restored to its original state with just a tap in the Photos app. To do this, just locate the edited item, and press "Edit" at the base of the screen, and then press "Revert.

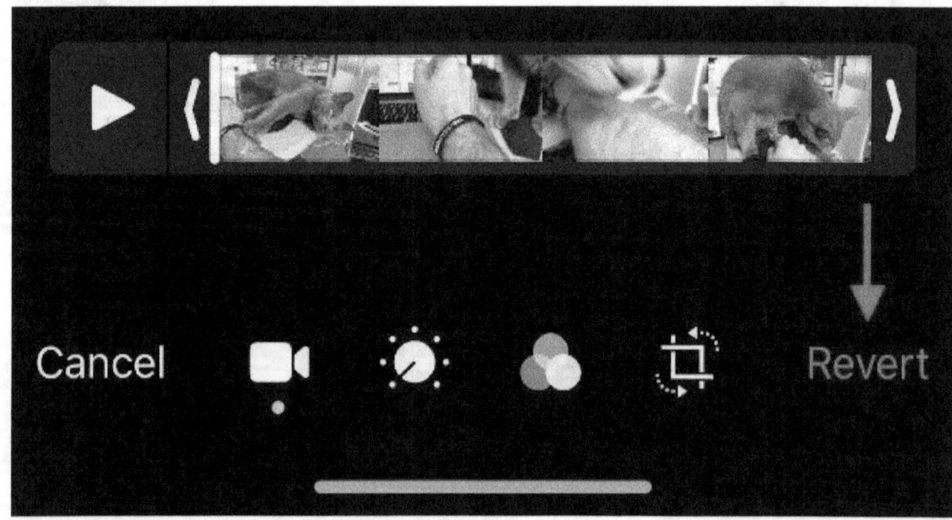

How to record 4k selfies

Perhaps you are a vlogger or a person who relies so much on high-quality selfie camera footage, the 4k selfie feature is of high importance to you. Apple's most recent iOS devices are all embedded with a 4K front-facing camera, and the video quality is something to write home about. Having stated that, the video won't be in 4K by default, the resolution has to be set by you. Let's get to how you can change your video resolution settings so the 4k video feature is enabled. Go to Settings on your device and select Camera –> Record Video. In this page, you can select your intended resolution and frame rate:

4K at 24 fps

4K at 30 fps

4K at 60 fps

Basically, the lesser the frame rate, the less the data that will be consumed by your video. That being said, those three options will consume 135 MB, 170 MB, and 400 MB per second, respectively.

 You can confirm that you've successfully converted your resolution to 4K if you check your resolution and frame rate in the top edge of the camera screen.

Disable Attention Awareness feature

Sometimes, you might observe that your device does a few things automatically if you're taking a glance at it. For instance, your screen won't dim if your face is still directed towards it and your ringer's volume will decrease the moment you're facing the screen as well. The cause of this is the Attention Awareness feature on your device. By deactivating this Attention Awareness feature, you can put a halt to your alert noises from decreasing by itself and your screen will dim with your face directed towards it, which may help optimize battery power.

To do this, go to the Settings on your device and select General. In that page, press Accessibility, then choose Face ID & Attention.

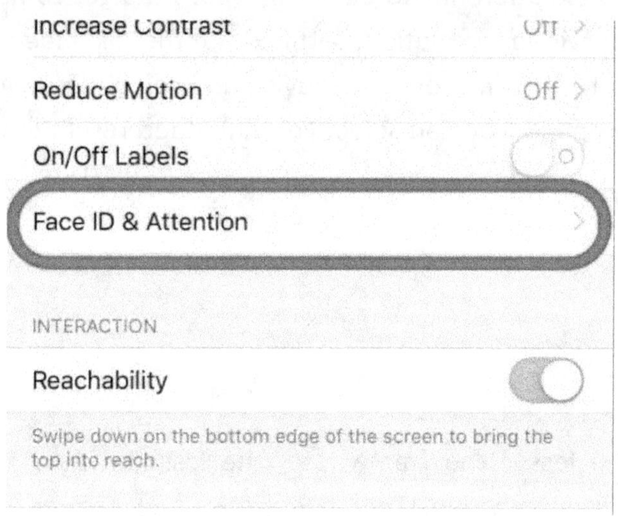

At this point, press the Attention Aware Features button to deactivate it.

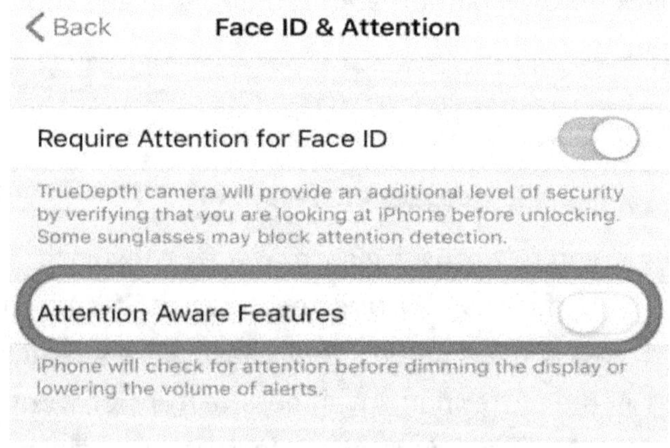

Well done! With that, you've gotten more control over your device's basic functions.

How to Enable or Disable Tap to Wake

Most Apple devices that run on iOS 14 have an inbuilt feature called Tap to Wake, just as its name implies, this feature enables the locked iPad screen to wake up with a tap anywhere on the screen. This seems to be very useful in the sense that most of these devices do not have a Home button which you can press and wake the screen. Therefore, tapping anywhere on the display kind of functions the same way that pressing the Home button functions, however Tap to Wake could also create a number of unnecessary screen waking, and by implication, any erroneous screen waking may have an effect on battery life.

Switch Control	Off
AssistiveTouch	Off
Touch Accommodations	Off
Side Button	
Siri	
3D Touch	On
Tap to Wake	
Keyboard	
Shake to Undo	On
Vibration	On
Call Audio Routing	Automatic

Nevertheless, a significant number of users prefer Tap to Wake because it seems to be convenient, however if this feature doesn't seem suitable to you or you're concerned about unintentionally waking the screen repeatedly, then it is advisable that you deactivate it. To do this, go to settings on your device and select "General", and afterwards press "Accessibility". In this page, scroll down and locate "Tap To Wake", you can then press the switch button to either activate or deactivate it.

How to set up Haptic Touch

Haptic Touch is a multi touch feature that has a very wide array of functions on iOS devices. With the haptic touch feature, actions can be launched via a long-press to rather than using the applications. Furthermore, with haptic touch, you can manage your notifications, handle messages and links, switch keyboards, switch apps, and so much more. Haptic Touch is a sort of wormhole through iOS that enables the user to do more without having to do more. Basically, haptic touch supplanted 3D Touch in iOS 13. A number of the functions have maintain their similarities, however, the way in which you arrive at those functions differ slightly. Users no longer "deep press" or "hard press" to initiate an action. Rather, you simply place your finger on what you intend to get more subtleties on or carry out a new task and hold it there for few seconds. Afterwards, select the action you want to use.

How to see Home screen actions with Haptic Touch

In order to display the Haptic actions for a particular app, you can press the app icon and hold your touch on it to bring up quick actions. The entire applications on your device are compatible with haptic touch, hence they have haptic actions, starting from the standard App Store app shortcut that enables you to share the app with someone else.

Certain applications have numerous quick actions, including dynamic quick actions that update based on the last person you communicated with, an article you perused, a movie you watched, etc. Press an action in an app's haptic actions so it leads you directly to that feature or content in the app.

For the basics, Long press (Haptic Touch) on the application icon you intend to open quick actions for, afterwards, select the action you intend to perform.

Dynamic actions function in a similar way just that only the subject of the task will be changed contingent upon the location, time, amidst other factors.

How to customize Haptic Touch

If Haptic Touch seems to be too complicated to be used for you, or you're having difficulty engaging it, you can make certain adjustments to the way it functions, one of which is adjusting the pressure sensitivity levels in Settings. You can test each setting by utilizing the peek and post demo below the setting. This will ensure that you get the best option.

Go to settings from your Home screen, and select Accessibility. Here, press the Touch option

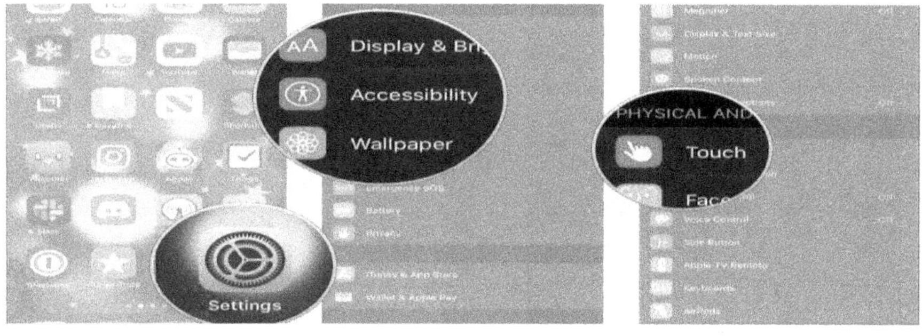

Now, press Haptic Touch and select Fast or Slow to alter the time it takes to initiate the Haptic Touch.

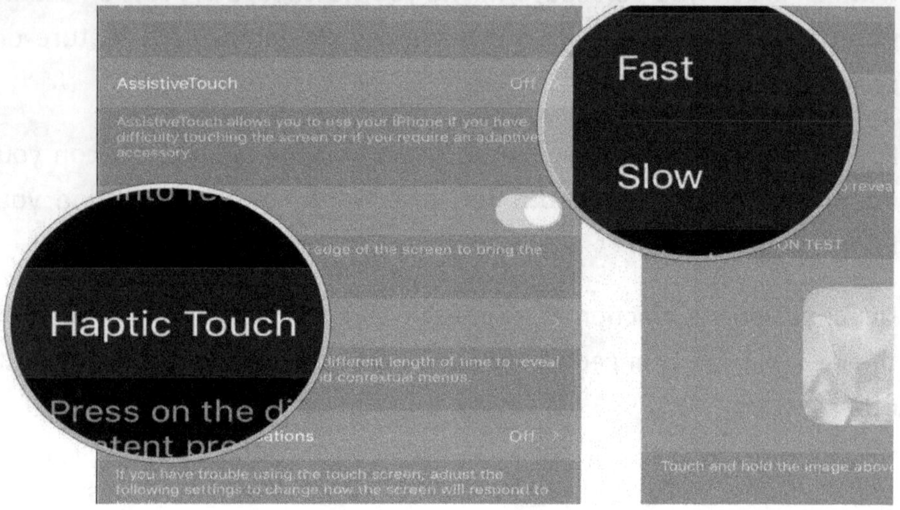

Chapter Eight

Features of Map App

The Map App is an inbuilt application available on all iOS devices. Asides its basic functions of helping the users find their way, it also has other features which users might, some of these are;

- Sharing directions on Maps from your Mac to your iPad

Perhaps you're utilizing the Maps app on your Mac to work out your planned trip, when you're set to go, you can just send the directions to your iPad. One thing you should note is that you'll must have signed in to an iCloud account using an exact Apple ID on both devices. Open the Maps app on your Mac, then press Directions. After that, input the location you're starting off from and where you're going. Now, press the Share button, the share button resembles a square with an arrow, positioned in the toolbar in the Maps app. Afterwards, choose your device, it should be displayed at the crest of the list. You'll then be notified on your iPad, press this notification to open it so the directions will be displayed on your phone.

Explore 3D mode in Apple Maps

3D maps are known to provide users with livelier scenes. Normally, when you're in Apple Maps, what you will see are buildings in 2D mode by default. However, this can be changed to 3D mode by placing two fingers on the screen and dragging upward. This is effective in both transit and satellite map views. You can get an improved view of the whole panorama of the buildings by zooming in and holding one finger down on the screen while moving the opposite finger across the screen.

Take the Flyover tour

Perhaps you're searching for a city in Apple Maps, you will be provided with the option utilize Flyover mode. Flyover mode enables you to view the city from the sky, and you can even zoom in closer to have a clearer view of the buildings. That can be helpful considering the fact that there are certain landmarks or alternate routes that can only be seen by having a wider and clearer view. To utilize this feature, search for that city and select Flyover. You can get a clearer and more detailed view of the buildings, roads or landmarks by zooming in and out on these items, be it the Statue of Liberty or the Eiffel Tower. Zooming on an item in Maps is done by pinching the screen. If you want to view different parts of the city, change the orientation of your phone by moving it up, down and sideways. Furthermore, you can as well view the surroundings of the buildings by holding one finger on the screen and moving it other across the screen.

Clear location history

In case you'll prefer not to have your locations logged, there is a way to implement that too as you can erase the places you must visit regularly and prevent Apple from storing those locations, your privacy is a priority.

Visit Settings on your device and select Privacy > Location Services > move down the page and press System Services. Now press Significant Locations, a form of authentication will be required at this point either by filling in your passcode, use FaceID or TouchID in order to proceed. With that, the areas you have visited will be displayed, as a matter of fact, details about the trip such as the number of times you've gone there and the amount of time it took you to arrive there.

To erase these records, scroll to the base of the list and press Clear History. However, what you've just done will not hinder Apple Maps from logging your location in the future, therefore, there is a need to go a step further and deactivate the switch off for Significant Locations, positioned at the top of the screen.

Place Card Events

- **How to create a calendar event on your iPad Air**

On your device, open the Calendar app and press the plus sign in the upper edge of the screen. Here, fill in a title, date, and time of your event. You can as well input an exact location if you wish.

Then, select whether you want the event to be regarded as an all day event, you should deactivate this option in case the event has an actual time. The dates and time will then be displayed which you can edit and change. In case it is a repeating event, you can customize it in the calendar to do so. You just press Repeat, and select how regularly you want the event to be repeated.

Now you can select whether you'd like to be notified when it's almost time for an event, and set the time you want the notifications to come in prior to the event.

Additionally, you can input a URL if there is a website related to your event. Then press Add so your entries are saved

- **How to edit a calendar event on your iPad**

Open the calendar app on your device and select the day on which the event is to take place. You may be required to select the year or month too, contingent upon the view your Calendar app starts from. Now, select the event that you intend to edit and press Edit at the edge of the screen. Carry out why changes you need to and then tap Done to save your changes.

- **How to delete a calendar event**

Open the calendar app on your device and choose the month or day that event took place, or is to take place. By default, the day will be marked by a grey dot. Select the event that you'd like to remove, then move down the page and press Delete Event.

In case it's a repeating event, you'll have to choose between " Delete This Event Only or Delete All Future Events".

Real-time Transit info

Apple has unobtrusively been making advances on its Apple Maps push around the world with numerous countries and US urban areas getting new and extended highlights as of late. Those highlights incorporate Look Around and real-time transit information. Apple has been working diligently on real-time transit information adding train, transport, and more open travel data to several places.

New US cities can now be partakers of this development of real-time transit data. Some of these US cities are:

Alaska

Atin (TX)

Baltimore (MD)

Burlington (VT)

California

Colorado

Dallas (TX)

Florida

Houston

Furthermore, Apple Maps also included support for Look Around to these US locations. This feature operates in a similar way to Google's Street View and permits users to view an area in 3D prior to visiting.

Expanding the span of this feature, Apple Maps is now compatible with the Nearby feature in more countries. This feature permits users to search for places or spots around their current location.

Furthermore, turn-by-turn navigation has also spread to numerous countries and islands, thereby decreasing users' reliance on third-party mapping apps for travel. These countries include:

Aland Islands

Anguilla

Aruba

Bahamas

Bermuda

Bonaire

British Virgin Islands

Cayman Islands

Chile

China

Dominica, etc.

Also, another embedded feature is the indoor mapping of airports with a large number of airports now listed as having been included.

How to create favorite locations

In the Maps app, you will see Favorites near the top of the screen. It entails your Home and Work location. Each Favorite entails the duration it takes to arrive at that place from your present location. To include a location to your Favorite, go to the Maps app on your device, and under Favorites, move the screen towards the right side and press the + icon. Now, fill in your location in the search box placed below Add Favorite. In that search box, you can type in a name or address. Still on the same page, you can as well press the Siri icon so it brings in the "Search with your voice" feature.

Next, press the + to include the location. You can then go ahead to change the title of the location if you want. In case you decide to share your location with anyone whenever you're visiting your favorite location, select Add Person under Share ETA. Then press Done at the top edge of the screen to save your Favorite.

You can also delete Favorites:

In the Maps app, press See All placed closed to Favorites, then select the information icon on the location you intend to remove, and press Remove Favorite at the base of the screen.

How to create Collections in the Maps app

Take for instance you're planning a trip to somewhere and you would like to identify and save areas of the city that you intend to visit. When you group everything in one location, you'll be conversant with those hotspots, and where they are situated even before you even arrive at your destination.

To create a Collection, open the Maps app and press "See All" placed towards the right side of Collections. Then select + at the base of the screen.

Now, give your collection a name or title, and press Create.

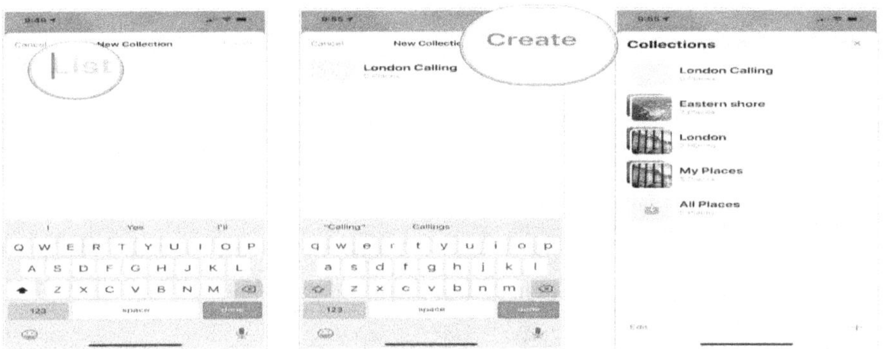

To add locations to a Collection, open that Collection and select press "Add a Place". Pinpoint the location by typing it into the search box, the location will then be displayed. Now, press the "+" placed near the location you intend to add.

If you want to add more locations or places to your Collection, search for them in the search box and press the "+" placed next to these locations. Afterwards, press Done at the edge when you are done including those locations.

- **Explore your Collection locations:**

You can navigate through your collection locations if you want to, it's quite easy to do, simply tap a location in that collection to view more details about it. If you intend to get a clearer view of the area, press Flyover. Perhaps what you want to know is how you can arrive at that location, press "Directions" .

Moreover, information sourced from Wikipedia and TripAdvisor will be displayed on the main location screen, depending on how popular the area is. Likewise, you can do other things from this screen, some of which are; adding that location to your Favorites, creating a new contact related to the location, bringing in an existing contact, etc. At the top of the location screen, you can bring in a location to another collection by pressing when you press Add. Also, you can share details about your location to other people either via messages or mails by pressing Share.

To exclude a location from your Collection, press Edit at the base of the Collections page in Maps. Then press the circle positioned towards the left side of the location you intend to remove, now press Delete to remove the location from your Collection.

Better CarPlay Integration

CarPlay was first developed about five years ago, and aside from being granted the ability to utilize third-party mapping apps a few years, it hasn't really changed since then. However, with the introduction of iOS 13, a couple of significant changes have been made to various aspects of the CarPlay app.

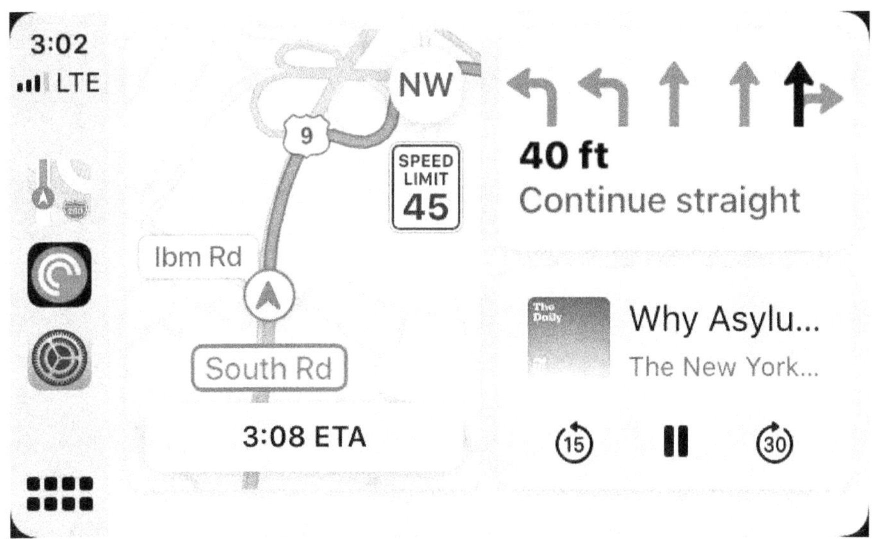

The greatest redesign in CarPlay App is its new multifunction dashboard. This permits you to simultaneously view a map, what's presently playing on the vehicle's sound system, and the next bit of direction to your destination all in one place. Before this upgrade, CarPlay required bobbing between two screens to see a track name while getting bearings to a direction. This upgrade makes it a lot simpler to see that data initially and afterward immediately set your eyes back on the road.

The New Dashboard Makes It Much Easier To Quickly Get Information

As far as CarPlay is concerned, Apple has upgraded its own Maps application broadly for, and those enhancements are seen in CarPlay. The new Maps application makes it simpler to get to your favorite destinations and gives better path direction on multi-path roads. Furthermore, iOS's new dark/light theming modes are accessible in CarPlay as well, however the default is the dark mode and the light mode is just accessible during the day, apparently due to the fact that it'd be excessively bright and distracting around evening time.

The interface has additionally been given updates like adjusted corners and an invigorated status bar, however outside of the new dashboard screen, the matrix of application icons stays as before.

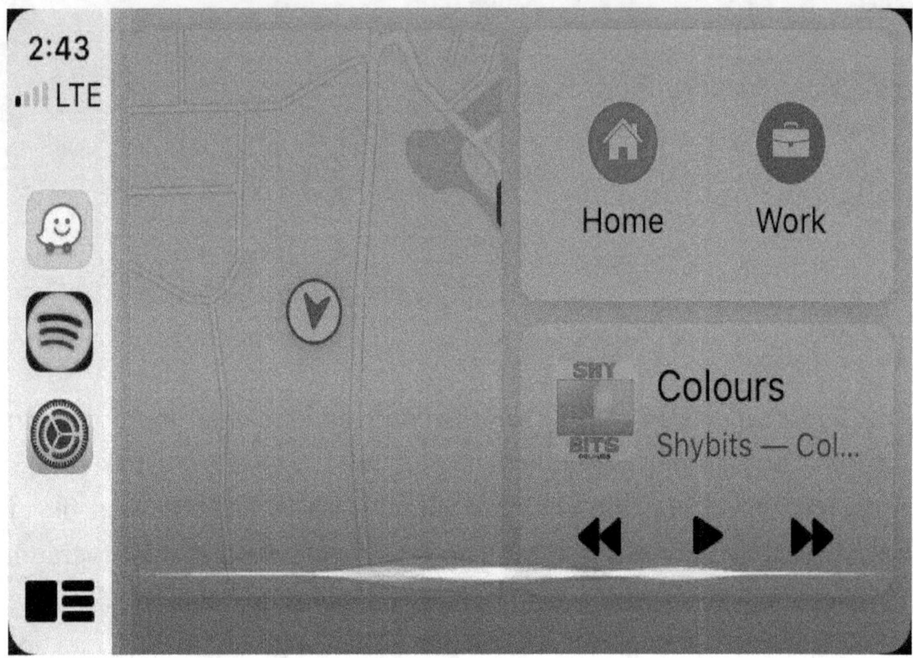

Also, Siri's interface is far less meddling than it was. Although, Siri behaves the same way it does in iOS 13's CarPlay, yet the interface for when you're addressing Siri and it's giving a reaction has been disentangled and doesn't show you out to an alternate screen. In case you're perusing a map and making an inquiry from Siri, you can in any case peruse the map, while Siri gives an answer. Siri will likewise give proposals in the new dashboard see for HomeKit-viable gadgets like carport door openers and will have the option to play music and other sound through outsider applications like Spotify or Pandora.

There's also another Calendar application for CarPlay, which lets you see forthcoming events and get headings to them or call participants with one tap. Beside the new dashboard, the standard lattice of application icons remains unchanged.

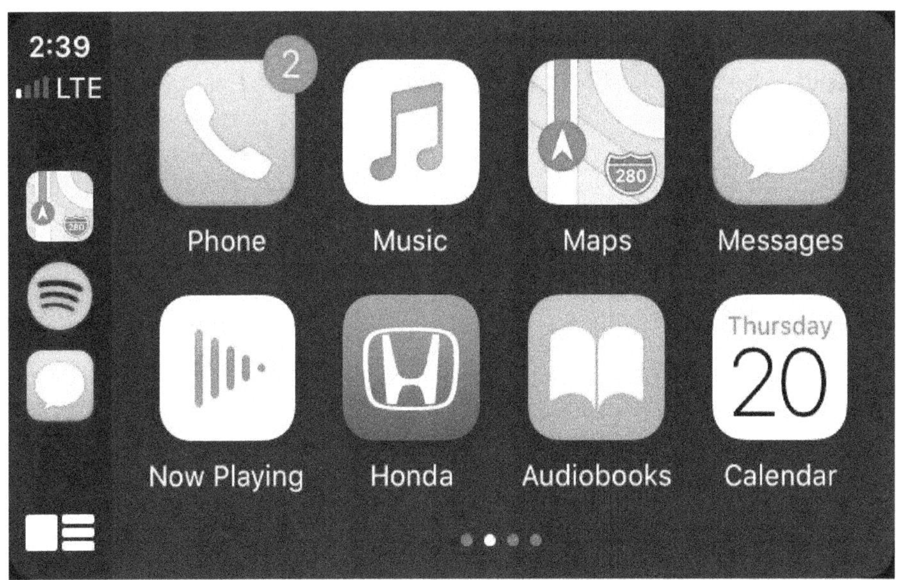

Carmakers will have the option to create mouthpieces that can generally tune in for "Hello Siri" orders, so you won't need to hold a button on your directing wheel or long-press the home button on the CarPlay screen to dispatch Siri. It's not yet certain about what precisely will be required for this to work, for instance, while testing this particular feature out, Siri would react to a "Hello Siri" order when it was quiet in the vehicle, yet it would not do so when any music or media was playing. That implies it's almost certain the mics on the iOS device were getting the voice order, rather than the vehicle's inherent receivers.

Carplay Now Lets You Control Apps Independently On the ipad Air

Additionally, CarPlay now takes into consideration the capacity to freely control an application on the tab that is not the same in relation to the one being shown in the vehicle's screen. Preceding this, whenever you utilized the phone to do something while you're using CarPlay in your car, it would close the screen that is being shown in the vehicle, which made it baffling for travelers to attend to something or read something on the phone itself. Presently, with this upgrade, you can utilize the iPad Air 4 for any application and the CarPlay session will stay continuous.

Chapter Nine

Making a Record in Voice Memos

Creating a record in voice memo is quite straightforward, you simply open the Voice Memos app on your iPad and press the record button to start the recording. The recording initiates with a graph, which displays the audio levels. After you're done recording, tap the record button to halt and save the recording. On the other hand, you can simply press the recording so it will be displayed in full screen. When it is placed in this mode, the recording can be paused and continued later, then press Done to stop and save the recording.

Trimming a Recording

To trim a record implies that you're removing certain parts of that recording, press the crop icon positioned at the top edge of the editing screen. This will provide you with other options. Trim excludes the sections of the audio that are before the left yellow indicator and after the yellow indicator positioned on the right side. If you press Delete, it removes the entire Audio enclosed in these yellow indicators.

Furthermore, on the yellow graph that is situated at the lower portion of the screen, you can adjust the left indicator to the starting position and move the indicator on the right side of the terminal position. Afterwards, press either Trim or Delete, contingent upon whether you intend to remove the sections that are outside or inside the two indicators

Before finalizing this task, play the audio in order for you to be certain that you trimmed the intended aspects. If this isn't the case, cancel it and carry out the trimming again till you're satisfied with the changes and then you can save it.

Edit Recordings

You can as well make edits to a particular audio in case anything comes up. Press the crop icon on the editing screen. What Trim does is to remove to cut out the aspect of the audio before the left yellow marker and after the right yellow marker. While Delete completely excludes the audio present in the two yellow markers. A yellow graph will be displayed, move the marker on the left side to the starting point of the audio and move the marker on the right side to the ending position. Afterwards, press either Trim or Delete, depending on the content you intend to remove.

It is advisable that you play the audio to verify that you removed the intended section. If otherwise, cancel it and do it again till the intended sections are removed, then you can go ahead and save it

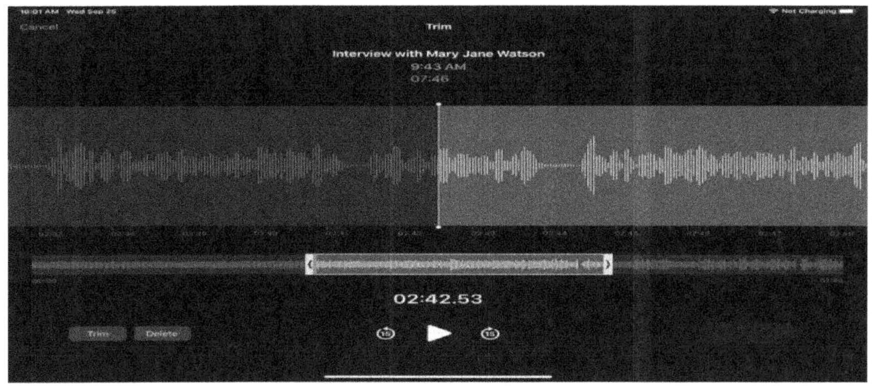

Share Recording

Subsequent to finalizing your recording, you can perform certain actions such as copy, share, or duplicate it. Press the More info icon (•••) for that recording to view these options. If you want to create an M4A file of your recording, press the Copy icon, then press Share to send the recording to other people through email or messaging app. Also, you can duplicate the file to Box, Dropbox, Google Drive, OneDrive, or another storage site. Afterwards, select Save to Files to save it to any service set up through any of these aforementioned iOS Files apps.

Moreover, there is a provided link to Edit Actions which allows you to enable or disable certain actions from the menu, these actions include Save to Files and Save to Dropbox. Likewise, you can as well adjust the arrangements of these actions. Normally, the actions that you classify as Favorites appear at the top of the list. Bring in the entire actions to your Favorites, then press and hold on its hamburger icon to alter their positions on the list my moving them.

Replace Audio

You can as well replace an audio after recording it. To do this, press the Edit link at the edge of the screen. Now, move to the start point or the area you intend to replace and tap the Replace button so it records a new audio portion. When you're done recording the replacement audio, press Pause to put a halt to it. Now you can go back to the beginning of the section you replaced and listen to the new audio, press Done if you're satisfied with the changes.

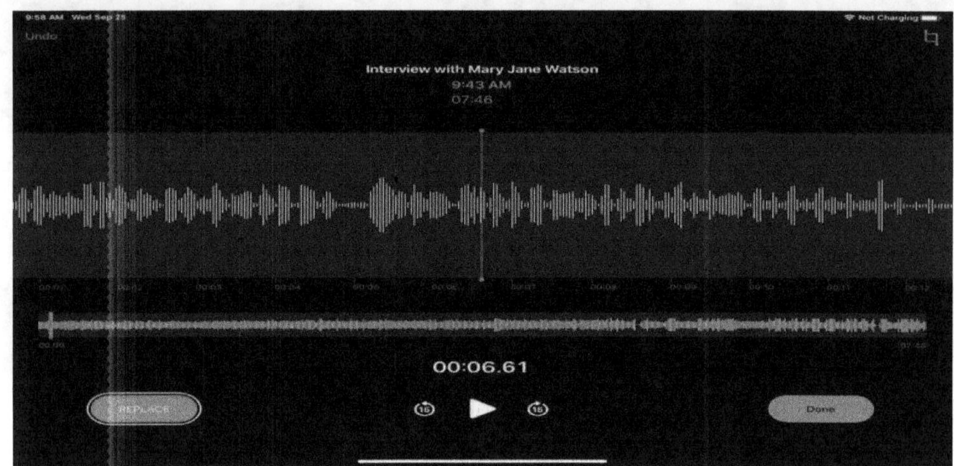

Deleting and Recovering a Record

To delete an already saved record, tap the trash can icon next to it, and that does it. However, if you're in the record's screen, you can simply press Delete at the top of the screen.

To recover a record you deleted, go to Recently Deleted in the Recording App and select the recording. Next, press Recover and then select Recover Recording.

9:56 AM   Wed Sep 25
Not Charging
Back
Edit
Recently Deleted
Interview with Mary Ja...
9:43 AM
07:46
Recover
Delete
Interview with Mary Jane Watson
9:43 AM
07:46
00:00.00

Chapter Ten

What is a Memoji?

A Memoji is another kind of Animoji that can be modified to look simply like you. It's as fun and exciting as it sounds. Like an Animoji, it utilizes Apple's facial tracking feature, however as opposed to being a unicorn or a robot, you can make it look simply like you. Everything about a Memoji is completely adjustable. You can customize everything down to the littlest detail, from your hair tone to spots. You can likewise mess around with it. You can attempt an alternate look or even make it resemble your favorite celebrity

Need to look somewhat more youthful? There's a choice to determine age too. Beyond physical attributes, there's an enormous selection of earrings, headpieces, caps and eyewear. The coolest part is that you roll out all the improvements continuously, so in the event that you don't totally like how your Memoji is ending up, you can make changes on the spot.

How is a Memoji made?

Most recent models of iOS devices have forward facing cameras that sense profundity, which implies it catches your facial movements and does this magical animation. It invigorates the emoji to look precisely like you dependent on your selections of features that represent you the best. Do you intend to make yourself look like someone else? This can also be done with your Memoji

How to Create Memojis

First, open a new or existing message, press the App symbol, at that point tap the Animoji icon, which resembles a monkey

Swipe towards the right side until "New Memoji" is displayed. Afterwards, press the addition sign to begin your new design

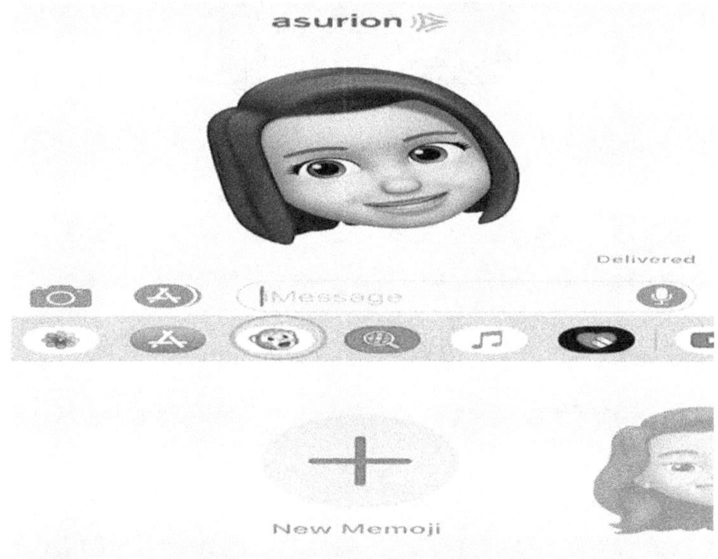

How to Edit and customize your Memoji

Tap through each segment to view diverse skin tones, hairdos, and facial highlights, check the lower part of each segment to add choices like spots, eyelashes, earrings, and beards. The customization looks more personal if you utilize an eyewear or a cap.

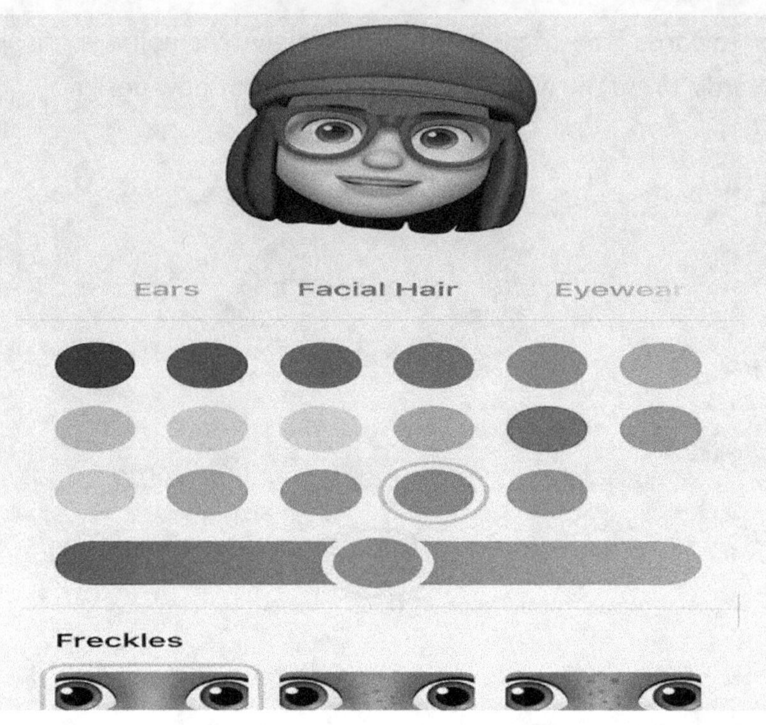

To change tone, pick an alternative and drag the slider from left to right. You can tap the shading wheel for further options. When you're satisfied with what you've created, tap Done. Your Memoji will be added to your collection of Animojis.

How to delete a Memoji

To erase a Memoji on your iPad Air, open Messages and go to any of your discussions. Here, press the Animoji button at the lower part of the screen and select your Memoji.

Tap the More info icon (•••) in the left corner, and press "Delete" to remove that Memoji

How to adjust Screen Brightness

Your iPhone or iPad is efficient at automatically adjusting its screen brightness based on how illuminated your surrounding is. Nevertheless, you might prefer to adjust its brightness by yourself atimes. Here's how to do that;

The quickest and easiest way to adjust the screen brightness is from the Control Center. You simply swipe down from the top edge of the screen on your device. The Sun icon/Brightness slider is placed next to the Sound icon/Volume slider.

Now, move the slider up or down, increase or decrease the brightness respectively. If the slider looks too tiny for you to control, press and hold the brightness bar to enlarge it.

On the other hand, you can as well adjust screen brightness in the "Settings" app. Simply go to Settings on your device and press "Display and Brightness."

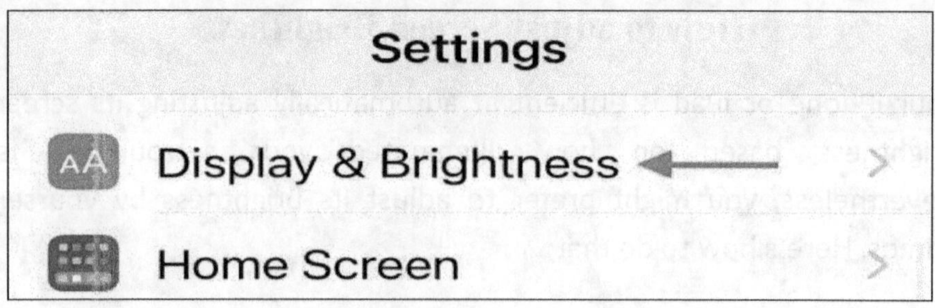

This will provide you with the brightness slider, swipe it to the left or right to decrease or increase the brightness respectively. With this manual setting, in as much as you're in the same lighting environment, the brightness level will be retained. However, if the Auto-Brightness feature is activated, it will by itself alter the brightness contingent upon the ambient light if you enter a different environment.

How to enable/disable Auto-brightness

Basically, auto-brightness is a feature that is embedded just to optimize your battery life and enable the users to read the iPad's screen more easily. For instance, let's say you're in your room at night with the lights off, the screen will automatically dim. Meanwhile when you're in a brighter place, maybe outside your house on a sunny day, it'll crank itself up to maximum brightness. Auto-brightness is very much useful in terms of adapting to dynamic circumstances, and since the screen is one of the major battery drainers on your phone, it is advisable that you enable the auto-brightness feature. Nevertheless, if you prefer to control the brightness manually, here's how to disable it

Go to Settings > General > Accessibility > Display Accommodations. Press the Auto-Brightness switch to disable it, pressing it again enables it.

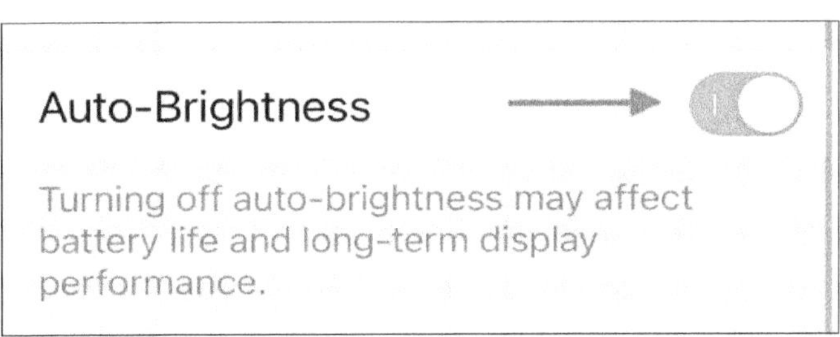

With this, your device's screen brightness will retain its level irrespective of the illumination level of your location.

Chapter Eleven

The Family Sharing feature on your device enables you to do quite a number of things, for instance you can share the entirety of your iTunes and App Store purchases with your family, even at that, you can set such that younger wards have to seek permission before they go ahead with any purchase. Furthermore, you can go through with a request and either accept or deny it right from your own iPad.

Here's how to go about Family Sharing feature;

To start with, there's a family organizer, who is the person that is basically expected to set up Family Sharing. The family organizer is tasked with receiving requests for purchases and giving consent to authorize the payment of any purchases made by anyone in the family group, adult or child.

To do this, go to the Settings app on your iPhone or iPad, and press the Apple ID banner positioned at the top of the screen. Then press "Set Up Family Sharing"

Afterwards, select **Get Started** and proceed. From here, you can include a photo beforehand if you want to, this is, however, optional. At this point, press Continue to share purchases.

Here, verify the payment settings and move on, any decision you make here can be changed later in Settings, so there's no need to worry. Now, press **Share Your Location** in order to keep your Family members posted about your location. You can then bring in family members. You do this by inputting the person's name and adding them

Next, input the credit card security code when required just to verify that you're the organizer. And that's all there is to it, you can keep on including new members until you get to the maximum number, which is 6. An email notification will be sent to them as a push notification on their devices inquiring if they want to accept your invitation. The moment they accept, the entire purchases made from that point forward will be charged to the family organizer's account. And they'll immediately be able to access the purchases of everyone else in the group.

How to accept a Family Sharing invitation on iPad

Perhaps the family organizer has sent you an invitation and you want to accept that invitation so you can become a member of the group, how do you do that? Here's how to: Open the settings app on your device and press the Apple ID banner at the crest of the screen. Here, select Invitations, typically, a number 1 person should be displayed beside it, except if you have other pending invitations. Press accept and proceed.

The next screen requires you to confirm certain details, you can alternatively choose a different Apple ID by tapping "Not (your name) or want to use a different ID?"

Go ahead to share purchases, and select whether you intend to share your location details or not.

Set Up Screen time for your Child

Parenting children in the era of technology comes with various challenges. One, which is ensuring that your wards are safe and healthy by restricting the time they spend staring at a ipad's screen. Also, it's paramount that you monitor what they are doing while they're active on these devices. With the Screen Time feature, this objective can be achieved and your family's device usage can be kept in check.

How to set up Screen Time for your child through Family Sharing

You can come up with a new Apple ID for your wards with Family Sharing. By implication, the entirety of your family members will be able share their Apple purchases such as apps, music, and books. Hence, you can put in place a Screen Time for each individual member present in your Family Sharing group.

Subsequent to including your child's account to Family Sharing, you can be in charge of their Screen Time settings by doing this:

Visit Settings on your device and press your Apple ID. Next, press Family Sharing and select Screen Time.

How to set up Screen Time for your child directly on the device

Family Sharing isn't the only way you can utilize to set up Screen Time, you can as well do it directly on your device. This method is even more preferable if you don't want to give your children their own Apple ID just yet and you want to put a Screen Time in place for them. Here's how.

Visit Settings and select Screen Time. A loss of insights provided by the Screen Time will be displayed, press continue so you can proceed.

Now, you'll be provided with a number of options, from this, select " This is My Child's iPad" in order to set up Screen Time on that device for a child. Then you can fix a Downtime, probably nighttime when you don't want them stuck on their device.

Start it and choose a start time and an end time, then press Set Downtime to save your settings.

Moreover, you can as well determine the amount of time per day that child spends certain applications on that device via app Limits. Take for instance, in a situation whereby you want them to spend just 30 minutes per day playing games, press Games to select that category. Then go to the base of the page where it states Time Amount, fill in 30 minutes, and press Set App Limit. This can be done on numerous individual applications from different categories..

Now that you've successfully set up the Screen Time on your child's device, it's time to wrap up the whole process so it becomes effective. Peruse the Content & Privacy controls and after that, fill in a four-digit Parent Passcode via the numerical keyboard. And here's how it works, when the set time is up, your child's device will demand this passcode in order to grant them additional time or to alter any Screen Time settings.

And that is all! The Screen Time settings on your child's device are now fully effective. In case you ever want to make any adjustments, simply go to the Screen Time page, input your Parent Passcode and make the changes.

Restrict Access to websites

Perhaps you just want ensure that you're not exposing your child to the inappropriate stuffs, and you just want to try to prevent them from hitting links that direct them to adult material, or there are certain sites you do not want them to even have a glimpse of, you can utilize the automatic settings and the blacklist feature. However, prior to putting this in place, you must have set up Screen Time on that device.

Open the settings app on your device and go to Screen Time. Afterwards, press Content & Privacy Restrictions.

Press the Content & Privacy Restrictions button to activate it, then select Content Restrictions. Next, select Web Content and press Limit Adult Websites.

Get a report of your device use on iPad

With the Screen Time feature active, you can obtain a report of how your device has been used. Open the settings app on your device and select Screen Time. Then, press See All Activity, afterwards choose any of these options;

Select Week so it displays a summary of your weekly use.

Select Day in order to view a summary of your device daily use.

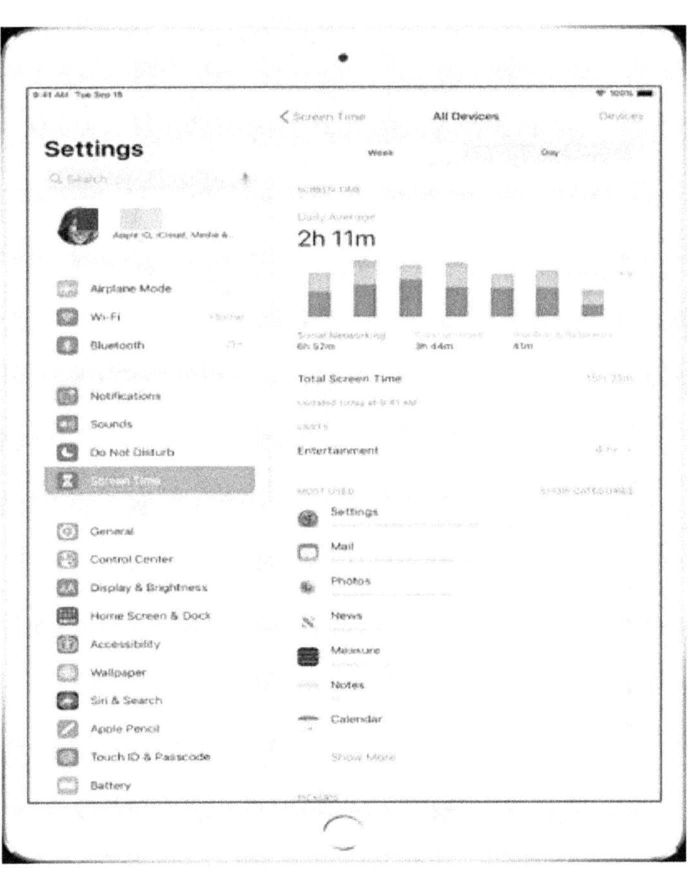

9:41 AM Tue Sep 15
Settings
Screen Time
All Devices
Devices
Week
Day
Daily Average
2h 11m
Total Screen Time
Entertainment
MOST USED
Settings
Mail
Photos
News
Measure
Notes
Calendar
Show More
Airplane Mode
Wi-Fi
Bluetooth
Notifications
Sounds
Do Not Disturb
Screen Time
General
Control Center
Display & Brightness
Home Screen & Dock
Accessibility
Wallpaper
Siri & Search
Apple Pencil
Touch ID & Passcode
Battery

Chapter Twelve

How to change your wallpaper on iPad Air 4

Outwardly, most iPad appear to be identical. However, as it is commonly said, what makes a difference is within. Of course, you can enclose your iPhone in a case, yet the quicker method to add to its aesthetics is by customizing your Home screen with a wonderful wallpaper. You can decide to add a default wallpaper made by Apple or utilize your own Photos application.

To start with, we should figure out how to change the wallpaper on iPad and utilize Apple's stock library. There are numerous choices for you to select from. In addition, a few backdrops change in case you're utilizing Dark Mode. Dispatch Settings on your iPad, look down and tap on Wallpaper, and select any wallpaper of your choice.

Tap on the type of wallpaper you want to use.

Dynamic: This refers to an image that is taken from Apple's stock photo library with effects that diminish into view and are sensitive to the orientation of your device.

Stills: These are still images that emanate from Apple's stock photo library.

Live: These wallpapers display a little bit of animation when you hold your touch on them.

Photo Library: An image that originates from your personal photo library.

Select from any of these categories and go into Preview mode. Here, you can decide whether you want the perspective zoom feature to be enabled or disabled. The implication is that if you enable perspective zoom, your wallpaper will move anytime you tilt your device.

Next, select how you want the wallpaper to function, maybe for your Lock Screen, Home Screen, or Both.

How to change wallpaper on iPad Air from the Photos app

Go to the photos app on your device and locate the picture you intend to use as your wallpaper and tap on it. Next, tap on the Share button placed at the lower edge of the screen.

Move down in the Share page and select the Use as Wallpaper option. Re-orientate your image to ensure it fits your screen the way you like it. Or set the perspective zoom option and set it. Now select how you want it to function whether for your lock Screen, Home Screen, or Both.

How to enable Reachability

A significant number of iOS devices have been embedded with a larger display, basically the days of utilizing one finger to carry out tasks are generally over. Nevertheless, it's still achievable, at least in a number of instances, with Reachability. When activated, the Reachability feature enables you to access items at the top of your screen by swiping down on the bottom edge of the screen to bring the top into a range where you can easily reach it. Here's how to activate this;

Visit settings on your device from the home screen and select Accessibility. Afterwards, move to the Physical and Motor section and activate the Reachability option.

How to add The Batteries Widget on the Home Screen

Another useful feature that comes with the iOS 14 is that users will be permitted to select a widget for any of the main screens that display your battery percentage always. Here's how to go about it;

Hold your touch anywhere on your Home Screen until the app starts to float, then press the plus button located at the edge of your screen. Next, go through the page until you locate the Batteries icon.

At this point, press the Batteries icon and check through to locate the Widget you want, when you come across the widget you like, tap on it.

Now put the apps and widgets in your home screen into order and press Done. And that is all! Check out your new Batteries Widget.

Offload Unused Apps on iPad Air

The Offload Unused Apps is a feature that enables users to remove Unused Apps from iPad, without having to lose the App's Documents & Data. It allows users to free Up Storage Space on their device by taking off applications that they haven't used for sometime, nevertheless they will still be able to re-download the Apps and start off right from where they left on the application. Contingent upon your decision, you can either set your device Offload Unused Apps automatically or you can Offload Apps by yourself.

1.   Automatically Offload Unused Apps on iPad

When the option to Offload Unused Apps is activated, it will automatically erase these Unused Apps only when your device seems to be short of storage space. Likewise, this option takes out only those applications that you haven't been active on for a while on your device. To activate this feature, go to Settings, move down the page and select iTunes & App Store. In the subsequent screen, move down the screen, here, you will see the Offload Unused Apps option, tap on it to activate it

What this does is that it automatically takes out the Unused Apps from your device, whenever your iPhone is devoid of storage space. Nevertheless, the applications you've offloaded will still retain their visibility on the Home Screen with a cloud icon placed next to them. These applications can be re-downloaded at any time by tapping on the cloud icon, and you'll continue from where you stopped

2. Manually Offload Unused Apps

Stick to these steps to manually Offload Unused Apps on iPhone or iPad;

Visit settings > General > Storage. Here, the amount of storage space occupied by different applications on your device will be displayed, as well as the previous dates on which you were active on these Apps.

You can then review the applications, and select the ones you intend to offload from your device. In the subsequent screen, press the Offload App option, and confirm your selection. For as many apps you intend to offload, repeat the steps above to do so. As stated earlier, offloading an application will provide you with additional amount of storage space occupied; however, the entire App related data will be retained on your device in case you want to use them at a later date, or if you later decide to re-download the App on your device.

How to move home screen apps on iPad

Each screen on the iPad can contain about 20 app icons, the moment that limit is reached, a new screen is added to your device. However, you don't have to wait till your current screen is filled up before you start to move apps to an alternate screen. Moreover, it is common among iPad users to manually move apps to another screen so as to group them together, for instance, the entire business apps can be put in one screen while the game apps are on another.

To do this, hold your touch on any app icon present on the iPad's home screen until all the apps start wiggling. Then, hold your finger on the app you intend to move, and drag your finger on the screen to move the app to another position. If you intend to open a new screen, drag the app towards the right side of the screen. Now you can release your finger from the iPad's screen to place the app in the new screen. You can do this for as many apps you intend you move to that screen. However, if you decide to move an application back to a previous screen, move the app towards the left side of the screen. When you're done with the moving and placing, you can press the "Home" button to lock the apps in place.

How to create a folder for apps on your Home screen

Creating folders on your home screen has an added advantage of making your apps more organized, easier to reach, and reduces the clumsiness of applications on your home screen. Here's how you can go about it:

Select the app and put it into edit mode. Then move the app icon you want to put in the folder, however if you intend to move multiple apps, you'll need to employ a second finger to tap each additional icon and place it in your folder. You just have to move the app icons such that they're on top of the last app icon to be moved and hold until the folder interface is displayed.

Snap out of the edit mode by tapping anywhere on the folder, then press anywhere outside the folder to take you back to the Home screen.

How to use the Find My app on your iPhone

Find My is an amazing feature on your iPhone that comes in handy when the need to use it arises. The Find My app can be used to track down any misplaced or stolen device and it works in a similar way to its predecessor, Find My iPhone. The Find My version however incorporates Find My iPhone and Find My Friends to provide users with one powerhouse of geolocation.

Here's how to set it up;

Go to settings from your home screen and select your Apple ID. In this page, press Find My, the switch then comes up and you can press it to enable it.

Another option you will be provided with is the ability to view your device location when it's offline by enabling Offline Finding. Also, if you want the location of your device to be sent to Apple when you have a low battery, activate Send Last Location.

In case your Apple Watch and your AirPods are interfaced with your device, they are automatically set up the moment you enable Find My.

How to find your iPad or other Apple device

The basic function of Find My is to assist in pinpointing iPhones, iPads, and watches that were misplaced, or stolen. The Find My feature operates with Location Services, hence to get started, go to Settings > Privacy > Location Services and enable the control. Furthermore, you can use Find My to have the misplaced or stolen device to play a sound, regardless of whether it was in silent mode the previous time you used it.

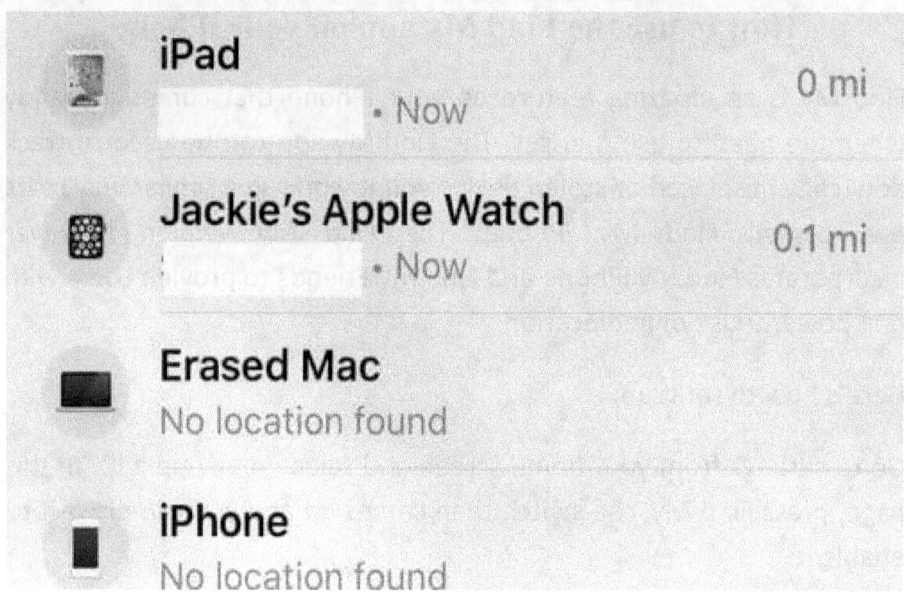

How to share your location

Interestingly, the Find My app permits you to share your present location with friends and family. The moment you open the app, it instructs you to enable Location Services and set the time this app can access your location, it could be any of these options: Allow While Using App, Allow Once, or Don't Allow. Allow While Using App is the most preferred option and has the most restricted usage, thereby causing the same message to show up every time you open Find My on your device. You can change this by going to Settings > Privacy > Location Services.

At the base of the screen, tap on the "Me" option that is displayed. The next screen is where you'll come across Share My Location, tap it to enable it. Afterwards, select the device you intend to share your location from, the thing here is that there are multiple devices from which you are allowed to choose one at a time. In situations whereby your location is shared from an iPhone or iPad that is paired with a GPS

Apple Watch, your location switches to the watch whenever it gets out of the range of your device.

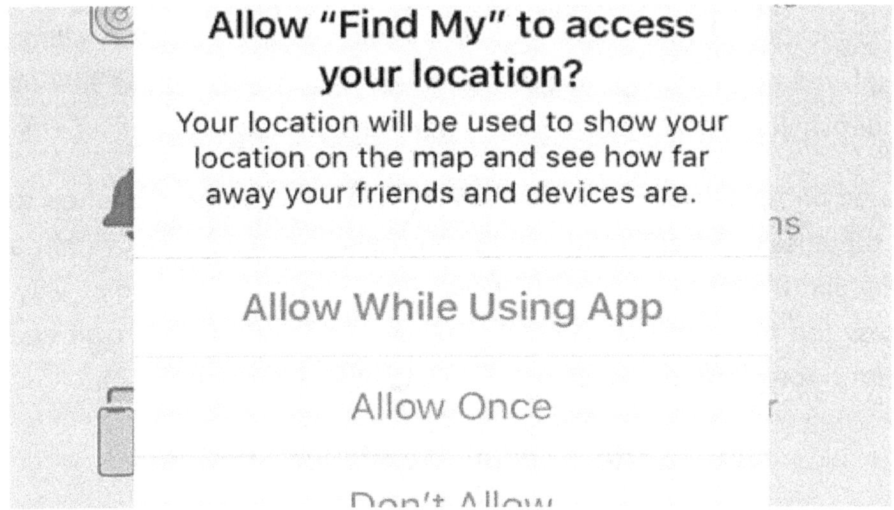

Moreover, this option can be easily deactivated if you want your location to be private. Also, sharing a location requires consent, therefore even if you decide to share your location, that doesn't mean the other person you are sharing with will in turn share theirs.

How to find family and friends

Additionally, the Find My app can be used to locate friends or family members, a feature that is synonymous to the previous Find My Friends app in previous iOS versions. To determine which contacts you intend to locate, your location has to be shared with them first, and if you want to view a friend's location, you must be invited by them from the Find My app on their device. Here's how to go about it;

Press the People tab positioned at the base of the Find My app and press the Start Sharing Location button. One thing Find My does is that it suggests contacts for you to share your location with, however anyone can be invited. After that, select the interval you intend to share your location, it could either be Share for One Hour, Share Until End of Day, or Share Indefinitely. Select any contact to view the details pertaining to that individual and request for a permission to follow their location. If your follow request is approved, their location will be displayed on your map. At this point, you can choose to quit sharing your own location if that's how you want it.

Based on Apple's designs, the Find My app has been programmed to automatically refresh locations for both people and devices within a very short interval of time, however if it doesn't function that way, press the name of that contact or device to display their card and refresh their location, or simply close and reopen the application.

How to add a task to Reminders on iPad

We are all bound to be forgetful regardless of whether it's a list of items you want to buy, tasks you intend to carry out, or just remembering to send some messages or make some calls. Luckily, the Reminders app is up to the task for reminding you of the activities you intend to do or complete. Starting off in the Reminders app requires you to include a task app. This task could be anything at all and can be in-depth or not, depending on how you want it.

Open the Reminders app on your device from the Home screen and select New Reminder. After that, fill in your task.

Alternatively, Siri can be used to bring in tasks to Reminders, you simply something like "Hey, Siri, remind me of the wash the dishes".

This is simply what has to be done in order to set up a basic reminder.

How to Receive Notification when sending messages via Reminder app

This feature is very useful in case you need to be reminded to perform certain tasks for a friend or family member, such as sending them a birthday card, or reimburse them using Apple Cash.

You can include a reminder to a list by pressing the New Reminder plus button present in a list. In case you are yet to create a list, press Today, Scheduled, All, or Flagged categories at the crest of the app screen and select New Reminder at the base of the screen. The moment you give your reminder a title, press the info ("I") icon placed next to it to display the Details screen, afterwards press the switch next to ``Remind me'' when messaging to activate this feature.

Select any Person you come across under that option whom you'll be sending a message to. After that, you can now go ahead and press Done at the edge of the Details screen and your reminder is good to go. From now on, the reminder notification will be displayed at the top of the screen at subsequent times of chatting with the person in the Messages app.

Remove Reminder

After the reminder app has served its purpose, and you carried out those activities or you attended the event, it instructed it to remind you. So, now, that whole list of tasks is no longer relevant, hence rather than cluttering up Reminders with lists you don't need anymore, you can simply delete them.

Open Reminders on your device and swipe the list you intend to delete towards the left side of the screen. Then press Delete. Additionally, you can erase a list, which was shared with you by someone at any time, to remove it from your devices.

Chapter Thirteen

Enable/Disable Swipe Typing on ipad Air

Start by opening the "Settings" app, then move down the page and select "General."

Here, you just tap on "Keyboard". Next, press the "Slide to Type" button to either activate or deactivate the swipe keyboard feature.

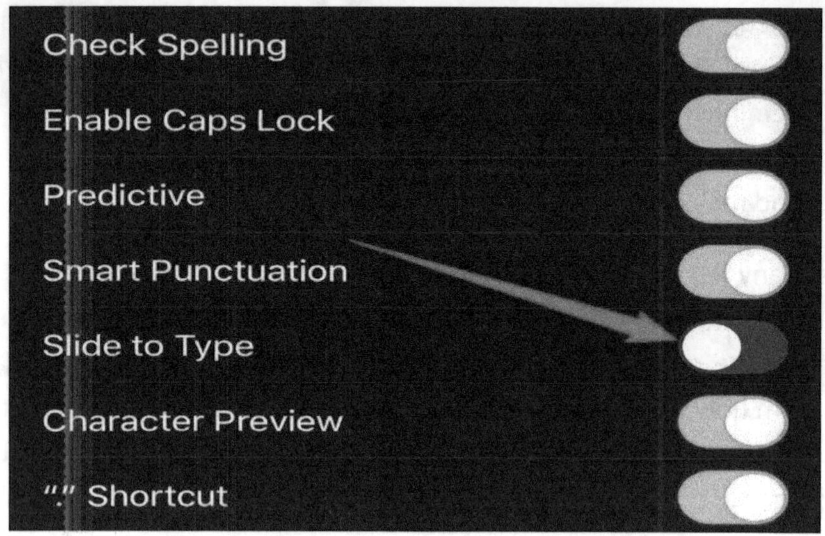

How to Use Swipe Typing

Swipe typing is a method of composing texts on your device without having to lift your finger from the keyboard while pressing the keys. It is particularly useful in situations where you're typing one-handed. Actually, it is faster than two-handed typing due to the much higher blunder rate that comes with using your thumbs. This brings us to a term called QuickPath, this is Apple's fancy name for its rendition of the swipe-to-type keyboards. Although some people refer to it as glide typing or slide typing, they all refer to the same feature. Moreover, using QuickPath might require some amount of practice, but it becomes very intuitive the moment you become conversant with it.

By default, the QuickPath feature cannot be used on the full width iPad keyboard because moving your finger across the whole keypad screen of the iPad wouldn't be convenient. However, what you can do is to use QuickPath by enabling the abridged floating iPad keyboard, which you can drag to reposition. To implement this, pinch inward on the default full-width iPad keyboard screen, just the same way you do when you're zooming in. When you do this, a similar but smaller keyboard which can be dragged around your screen, and swipe typed on will be displayed. To bring back the larger keyboard, simply pinch outward on that miniature keyboard, as if you are zooming out.

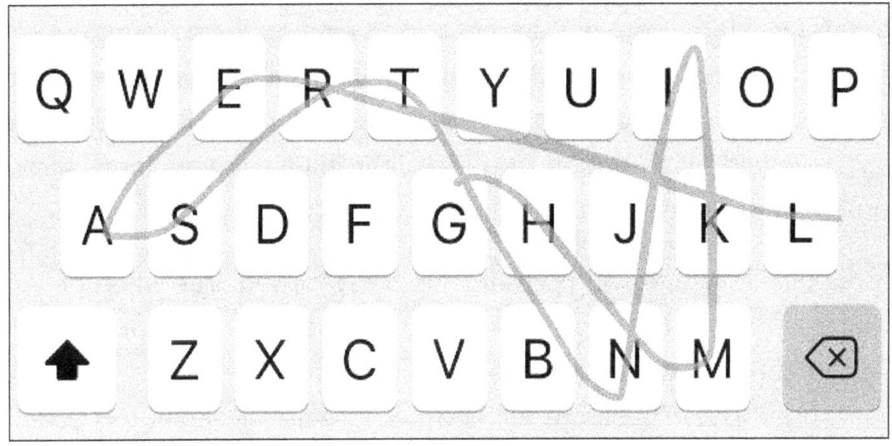

How to set a custom name and photo through the Messages app

This can be done directly from the Messages app, which is way more convenient when you want to swap or set pictures very quickly. Nevertheless, there is a little more that has to be done when you're setting it up for the first-time setup, however it becomes much easier afterwards.

Open the Messages app on your device and press the more info icon to provide you with an additional option. At the base of the screen, a button will be displayed, this button states Edit Name and Photo, press that button. On doing this, a subsequent screen will show up, this one states that states Share Your Name and Photo with Friends. Move to the lower part of this page and press Choose Name and Photo.

The next menu that will be displayed is where you can now choose your name and photo. First, fill out the two slots for your first and last names.

As soon as you fix an initial image and name, this interface again won't come up again. At this point, you will be provided with a number of options. At the crest of the page, there are big, circular icons that represent different options, and you can swipe on them from the right in order to view more. Also, in case you've initially made a Memoji or set your own photo in the Contacts app, these options will be displayed first, followed by an option to utilize your initials. If you come across something you like, press Continue.

An inquiry message will pop up, this message inquires whether you want the picture to be used everywhere, and your Apple ID and My Card in Contacts will be attached with this photo. If that is what you want, press Use. That's not all, another screen will show, this screen states "Choose Who You Share Your Name and Photo with." Here, you can decide to share with your contacts only. Hence iOS will consequently send the name and photo to the contact when you message them another time.

We're almost done, there's just a little more. Now, select Always Ask if you want iOS to request permission from you whenever it is about to send your updated name and photo to a contact. This implies that upon selecting this, the subsequent time you send a message to a person after you've made some adjustments to your information, a menu will be displayed at the top of the chat thread stating "Share your name and photo?" If you want to, press the share option and iOS will send them your information instantly. Go through with your selection, and press Done. That's all!

How to use the new gestures for cut, copy, paste, undo, and redo on iPad

The act of shaking your device in order to undo certain items mostly when typing hasn't been so on point for many iOS users, and it's kind of absurd for those who use iPad, however that is a bygone now as the recent iOS upgrades come with a vast range of alternatives which entails a new three-finger gestures. These new gestures aren't meant for only the undo and redo options, they also work for cut, copy, and paste.

Copy: copying an item is done via a three-figure pinch.

Cut: cutting an item out of a particular position can be carried out through a three-finger double pinch

Paste: simply place the three-finger on the item and pinch out, more like expanding it.

Undo: place the three fingers on the item and swipe left. An alternative to this is by double tapping with the three fingers.

Redo: place the three fingers on the item and swipe right.

Shortcut menu: you bring in the shortcut menu via a three-finger single tap

How to pair a DualShock 4 with an iPad Air 4

Open the Settings app on your device and enable the Bluetooth option. While you're still in the Bluetooth page, pick up your DualShock 4 controller and ensure it's charged. Afterwards, simultaneously press the PlayStation button and the Share button, and hold them down for a couple of seconds. The light emitting device located at the rear of your DualShock 4 starts to flash intermittently.

In the settings page on your iPad, what you will see is the "DUALSHOCK 4 Wireless Controller" showing up beneath Other Devices in the Bluetooth menu, tap on it. At this point, the light emitting device at the rear of your DualShock 4 would instantly transform into a reddish-pink color, this is a confirmation that your DualShock 4 is now paired with your iPad.

How to disconnect your DualShock 4 from your iPad

After pairing and you're done playing with the DualShock 4, here's how to switch it off and unpair it. Simply press the PlayStation button for about 10 seconds and that does it. Meanwhile, on the iPad, the quickest way to do this is via the Control Center. Simply open the control center on your device, you'll see the Bluetooth option. Hold your touch on the blue Bluetooth icon. This directs you to the Bluetooth menu. Here, what you will see is the "DUALSHOCK 4 Wireless Controller" among the options. Press it, and your controller will instantly get disconnected.

An alternative method is by opening the Bluetooth menu in the setting app on your iPad. The "DUALSHOCK 4 Wireless Controller" will be displayed under My Devices. Next to it is an info icon, press this icon. You will be provided with a menu, press Disconnect. This causes the controller to instantly stop working with your device. However, if you prefer to unpair the DualShock 4 instead, just press "Forget This Device" in the Bluetooth menu rather than Disconnect.

How to connect an Xbox One controller to your iPad

Switch the controller in pairing mode by simultaneously pressing the Xbox button and the pair button for a couple of seconds until the Xbox button begins to flash, denoting pairing mode.

Afterwards, go to the iPad's Settings app, and open the Bluetooth menu. It is important that you verify that your Xbox One console is not automatically connecting with the controller you intend to pair with your device, hence ensuring you switch off the console or be at a significant distance from the console. The controller will appear in the "Other Devices" section. As soon as it appears, tap it to pair with your iPad.

Chapter Fourteen

How to set up Voice Control on iPad Air 4

It's been demonstrated over and over that when technology turns out to be more available, innovation improves for everybody. Voice Control is another accessibility feature that lets pronounce orders to your iPhone or iPad. It's a colossal aid for individuals with restricted expertise, portability, and other conditions, but at the same time it's a phenomenal better approach to interface with your iPhone or iPad without hands. At the first time of using Voice Control, you'll have to set it up by adhering to these steps:

Open settings on your device and move to Accessibility, here, select Voice Control.

Next, proceed to the "Welcome to Voice Control" screen and move on. In the next screen, which is the screen that displays "What can I say?" Press continue.

-How to turn on Voice Control on iPhone and iPad

In as much as you've initially used the Voice Control feature, you can activate or deactivate it through these steps:

Open Settings on your device, move to Accessibility and select Voice Control. Here, press the Voice Control switch to either activate or deactivate it.

How to Block a Sender from Mail

The functionality of the blocking feature has been extended from the ipad and Messages app to the Mail app. To begin, open the "Mail" app, then locate the email from the sender that you intend to block. Next, select the Profile Picture to display the details of the sender.

Afterwards, press the name of that person in the "From" field. Hence, this will direct you to the sender's contact card. At this point, press "Block This Contact."

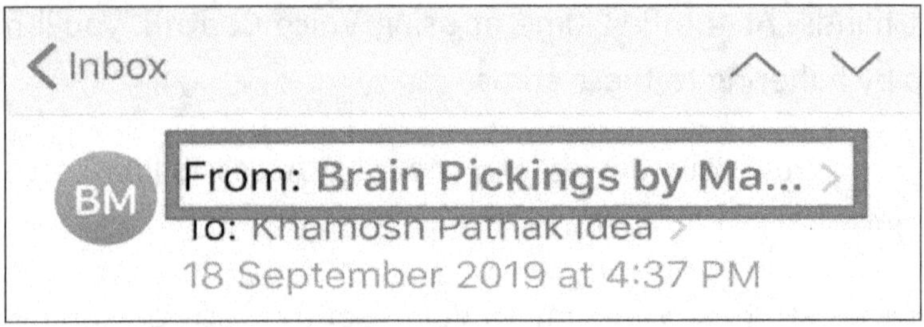

In the subsequent screen that comes up, verify your action by pressing "Block This Contact."

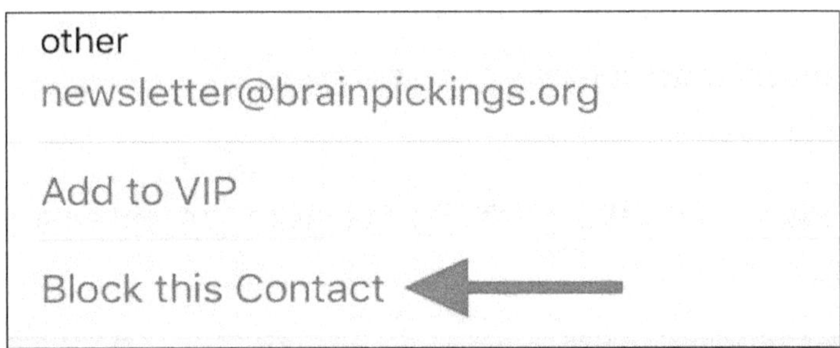

With this, the sender is now blocked. Anytime that person sends a mail, no notification will be sent to you. However, the messages will be shown in your Inbox with an icon informing you that it's from a blocked contact.

How to unblock a number or contact on iPad Air

To start with, you have to determine whether the contact or number you are unblocking is a number that is in your contacts, or just in your recent call list. Here's how to go about both;

- **Unblock a number in your contacts**

 Open the Phone app on your device and move to the "Contacts" tab. Locate that particular contact you're searching for and tap on it. Afterwards, move to the base of that contact menu view the "Unblock this Caller" option, and press it.

- **Unblock a number in your recent calls list**

Perhaps you blocked a number who called you recently and is not in your contacts and you want to undo that action of yours, here's how to go about it;

Open your Phone app, and Locate that number under the "Recent" tab. Then, press the info icon placed near that number. In this menu, move down and press "Unblock this Caller" and that is all.

How to add contacts on an iPad

Let's say you've just made a new friend or you ran into an old schoolmate of yours, and after the whole chitchat, you exchanged phone numbers, now you have to save that number and add it to your contact list. Here's how to do that;

Open the Contacts app on your iPad and press the plus icon placed at the crest of the screen in that app.

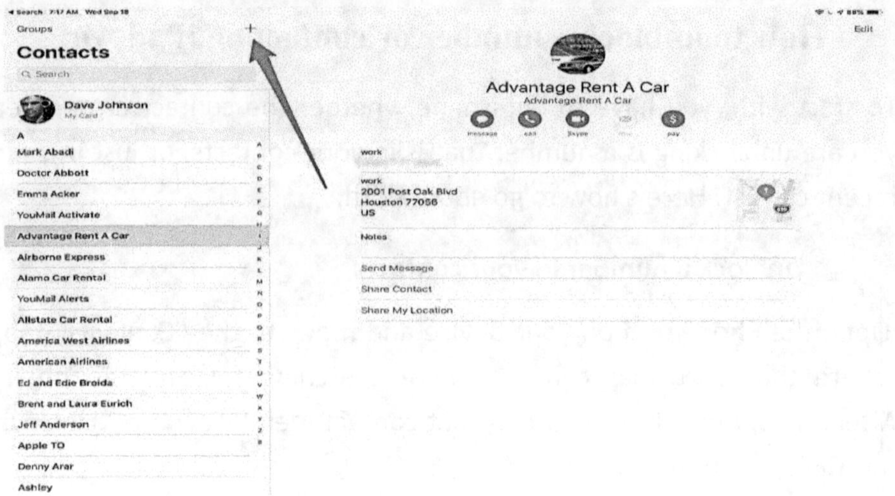

You will then be directed to a contact page where you can fill in the necessary details about the contact, this could be a whole lot of things ranging from the name, company, phone and email, and any other details you intend to include.

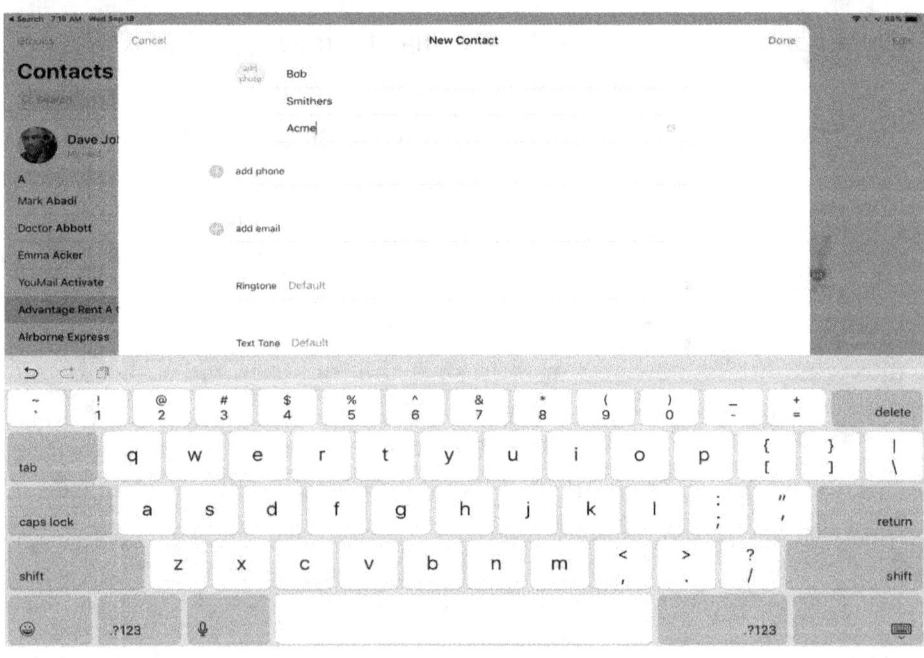

Perhaps you intend to assign a unique call or text ringtone to this contact, you can do that by pressing the default option close to the normal Ringtone or Text Tone field, then make your selection. Press "Done" at the crest of the screen when you are satisfied with the settings you've put in place.

How to set up voicemail

Visit the Phone app on your iPad, once you're in the app, press the voicemail icon positioned towards the right side of the base of the screen.

You will be taken to the Voicemail page which basically a void white screen is being the first time. Then, press "Set up now." In case the screen isn't empty, it implies that you've initially set up your voicemail and all these shouldn't bother you. Apple will then demand that you set a password, confirm this password and when everything is in place, tap Done.

With this, Apple will consequently take you to the Greeting page. At this point, you either select a simple default greeting in which you request that the caller should leave a message or you come up with your own message. If you choose to do the later, press Custom to record your own message, followed by Record to leave your greeting. After the whole thing, press Done.

How to Merge Duplicate Contacts

Bringing duplicate contacts together is typically referred to as "Link Contacts", here's how it works;

Open the Contacts app on your device and move to the contact you intend to merge with the others duplicate contacts, then press the

"Edit" button. Afterwards, move down the page until you locate "Linked Contacts". When you do, tap the green plus icon "(+) link contacts…" to merge this contact with another.

Now, go to the that other contact, it could be a duplicate or a changed addressee, and tap on the name, then select "Link" at the edge of the page

If there are other contacts, you want to merge with that particular contact, repeat the same process, and press "Done" after the whole merging process. By implication, the entire contact details from the two (or more) contact cards will be merged into a single contact entry, however no phone number, address or email information will be overwritten or affected, the entire contents are simply brought together into a single card.

The amazing attribute of the "Link Contacts" feature is that even though the contacts are merged from the user's perspective, the entire settings and merging can be easily undone if you decide to unmerge/unlink the contact details. To go through with this, just revert to the contact in question, press "Edit", then press the red (-) icon attached to the details of that linked contact.

How to turn on AirDrop for iPad Air 4

AirDrop is an embedded feature on iOS devices that enables users to swiftly and easily transfer files between Apple devices, be it an iPhone, iPad, or Mac. This feature utilizes a Bluetooth LE to transmit, explore and negotiate connections, and on-point Wi-Fi to transmit data. By implication, the AirDrop feature is fast, power-efficient, and very much secured. Various items on your Apple devices can be AirDropped, photos, videos, contacts, Passbook passes, Voice Memos, Map locations, and any other thing that you come across on the share list.

Furthermore, AirDrop provides you with the liberty of choosing whether you want the feature enabled for only your contacts or for everyone. The former, which is the "Contacts" option extra work, due to the fact that the person you intend to AirDrop a file with and you must be logged into iCloud and be in each other's Contacts.

 Bring in the Control Center of your device by swiping up from the bottom bezel, then hold your touch on the Wi-Fi button for a couple of seconds. Now, press AirDrop, and make your selection by choosing between Contacts Only or Everyone to activate AirDrop

How to AirDrop files from your iPad

Files can be AirDropped from any iPad app that bears the built-in Share page, and you can transfer these files to anyone and whichever of their devices that is displayed in the Share sheet.

Locate the item you intend to send with AirDrop, and press the Share button placed at the base of the screen (the share button has the appearance of a box with an arrow directed out of its top). Next, select the person or device you intend to share to. However, bear in mind that if your selection is Contacts Only, be sure that you're logged into iCloud. The reason for this is Apple won't share your contacts with a different device to ascertain if there's a match, rather what it checks is the two iCloud accounts. Afterwards, if there is a match, it'll display your own rendition of the contact present on your own device. In that manner, no data will be leaked.

However, if you're going with the Everyone option, despite the fact that you are very much visible to other devices, you will always be notified when someone attempts to share files with you through AirDrop. If you are not familiar with the sender or you've decided not to receive the files, you can always choose not to accept them. Files transmitted via AirDrop will be placed in the app that basically handles such types of files.

How to View Someone's Medical ID

Setting your Medical ID on your iPhone or iPad could serve as your lifesaver someday. It entails basic and significant medical information that pertains to you, which people can utilize, incase of an emergency, as well as a list of your emergency contacts. Here are some basic things you should know, including how you can locate the Medical ID on someone else's device during an emergency medical situation. There are numerous methods you can utilize to check the Medical ID on an iPhone/iPad, regardless of whether it's your device or someone else's.

Additionally, the Medical ID can even be accessed on a locked iPhone/iPad. Swipe up on the lock screen or simply press the home the home button, contingent upon the type of device you're using, this directs you to the passcode entry screen. Here, press Emergency > Medical ID at the base of the screen. Likewise, you can simply switch the Side button with either Volume button simultaneously, then slide across on the Medical ID option. As soon as the device is unlocked, go to the Health app and press the profile picture positioned at the edge of the screen, afterwards select Medical ID.

Incase the need to call emergency services arises, intermittently press the Side button or the Sleep/Wake button five times in a row. Doing this activates Emergency SOS and places a call through the emergency services available in your country. When you're done with the call, your device automatically sends a message to each emergency contact and displays the Medical ID.

What Is the Measure App?

The Measure app is an embedded feature on iOS devices that utilizes an augmented reality that enables users to draw lines that are exhibited as a graphical rendition of what the camera is displaying on the screen. What the Measure app does is that it converts these lines into actual measurements, which you can then snap, providing you with a record of the measured dimensions.

How to Take a Single Measurement with the Measure App

The Measure app on the iPad can be used in a similar way to the tape measure to carry out a single measurement. Here's how to go about it;

Open the Measure app on your device, it is a pre-loaded application on your iOS device and it resembles a ruler. The moment the app starts to run, it will instruct you to re-orientate your device, which causes it to calibrate distances on the surface you intend to measure. Ensure you keep the device pointed at the surface you intend to measure while moving it around. Direct the dot shown at the center of the screen at the starting point of the object to be measured, and then press the Plus icon on the screen.

Next, direct the point to the end of the measurement and press that Plus icon for a second time.

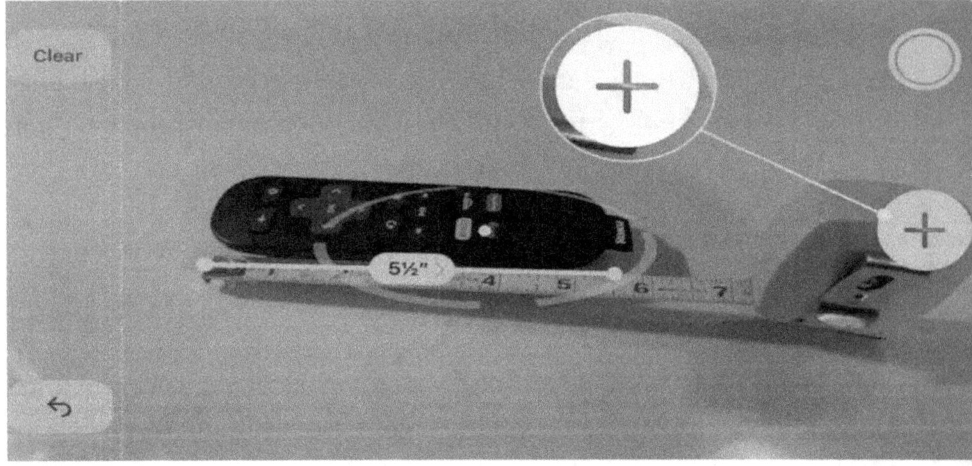

If there is a need for you to redo a measurement, press the Back arrow placed at the top edge of the screen to repeat the previous dot, or tap**clear** if you prefer to start from scratch. In case you want to copy the measurement details to your clipboard, tap the measurement to bring in dialog box, and then press **Copy**.

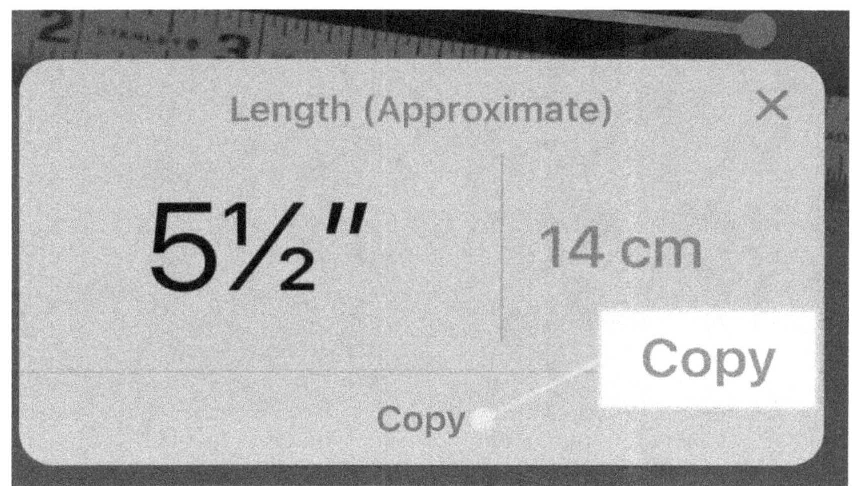

If, after the whole thing, you're satisfied with the outcome, press the Shutter button so as to take a picture of the scene that includes the measurement.

How to Measure the Area of a Rectangle With the iOS Measure App

In a situation whereby the Measure app identifies a rectangular object on the surface under the iPhone or iPad, it will automatically develop with a box around the object. If you want your device to automatically detect a rectangle, you have to be working in a well-illuminated environment and the object needs to tightly conform to a rectangular shape. In certain situations, the iPhone will not detect it and you'll need to carry out the measurements manually.

Consequently, the moment the Measure app recognizes that this object has a rectangular shape, if you still want to go ahead with this measurement, press the Plus icon and the measurements will appear automatically, alongside the area of the object.

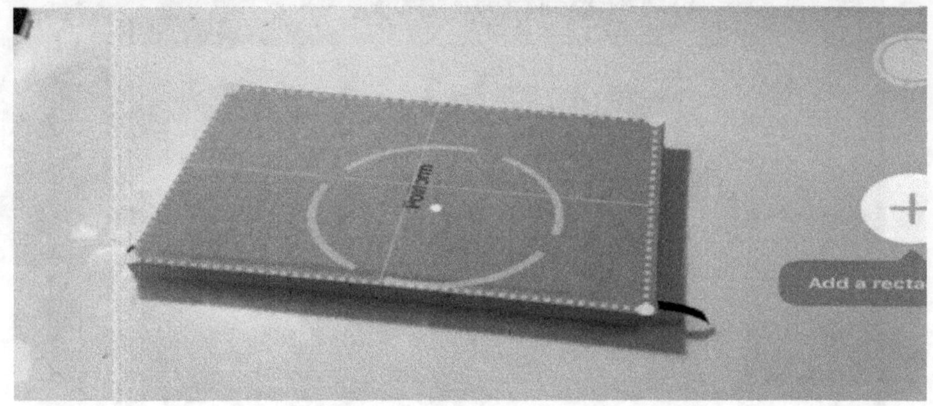

At this point, you can tap the area to bring in a dialog box that provides you with additional details about the measurements, as well as the diagonal dimensions related to the rectangle.

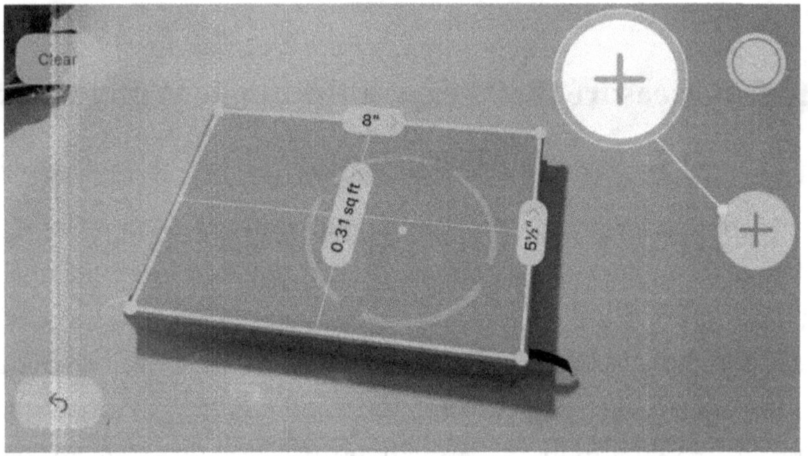

Conclusion

The iPad, particularly the iPad Air, is a top-notch device that every lover of a good gadget should endeavor to have. Its friendly user interface, as well as ease of use makes it a necessary buy for everyone who is a fan of iOS gadgets. In addition, just like the other iOS devices that have been released before now, the iPad Air provides you with that utmost utility and satisfaction that you derive from using a device.

About the Author

Daniel Stone is a tech expert with good expertise in reviewing the latest gadgets. He has written a lot of user manuals for Apple devices and computers. He read computer science from the University of Minnesota USA.